Onward Christian Road Warrior

Onward Christian Road Warrior

Avoiding the turbulence of the Adversary while traveling away from home and family

Matthew S. McNaughton

This book is a work of non-fiction. Names of people and places have been changed to protect their privacy.

© 2004 by Matthew S. McNaughton. All rights reserved.

No part of this book may be reproduced, stored in a retrieval system, or transmitted by any means, electronic, mechanical, photocopying, recording, or otherwise, without written permission from the author.

Published and Distributed by:

Granite Publishing and Distribution, LLC
868 North 1430 West
Orem, Ut. 84057
(801) 229-9023   Toll Free (800) 574-5779
Fax (801) 229-1924

ISBN: 1-932280-68-5
Library of Congress Catalog Number: 2004118392
Printed in the United States of America

To my wife, Kathy, and my six children, Matthew Jr., Shawn, Michelle, Katie, Morgan and Ashley.

ACKNOWLEDGMENTS

Over the past several years I have felt compelled to write this book. I'm grateful for my dear friend Ron Johnson, who one day walked over to my home and encouraged me to start the book. I am deeply thankful for Ron's encouragement, advice and support. I am also grateful for my wife Kathy and her constant support, love, patience and encouragement throughout the writing of this manuscript. Sincere thanks to my daughter Michelle for taking the time to review and edit a portion of my work.

A special tribute to the following individuals for their input, expertise, advice, counsel and support: Shawn McNaughton, Mark McNaughton, Austin McNaughton, Jon McNaughton, LaVar Christensen, Spencer Dunn, Marc Brown, Jan Johnson, Jeff Hochstrasser, Lynn Van Roosendaal, Dr. Tim Grace, Doug Anderson and Cary Campen. Special thanks to my publisher for receiving my work and piloting me through the process.

My sincere gratitude and eternal love for my parents Loraine McNaughton and the late Austin P. McNaughton.

WHAT PEOPLE ARE SAYING ABOUT
ONWARD CHRISTIAN ROAD WARRIOR

"I have known Matthew McNaughton for many years and have found him to be a master storyteller. I am delighted to see he has applied his skills to writing – this book is a must read for any Christian traveler in today's troubled world."
 – Ron Johnson, National Director, Telecommunication Company

"For any traveler who desires to return home with honor. This book contains effective principles and practical tips for avoiding the perils of the road. I highly recommend it!"
 – Marc Brown, Corporate Attorney for Fortune 500 Company

"Wonderful insights for anyone who travels either weekly or once a year. I found the tips useful, the stories entertaining and compelling. This is a must read for any traveler."
 – Monica Bradshaw, Pharmaceuticals Sales Representative

"Easy to read guidebook for the professional traveler. Practical ideas on how to increase your spirituality while on the road – based on true principles."
 – Dennis Vance, Commercial pilot with major airline

"I wish this book was written when I began my career 15 years ago as a traveling salesman. The principles taught in this book has changed the way I go about my travels. The stories shared are fascinating. This book is the most important travel guide I will ever own."
– A Reader from Seattle, Washington

"I love this book. Don't be fooled by the title – this book is for everyone. I highly recommend this book for all couples, especially those who spend time away from each other. Read this book with your spouse and watch your love, trust and confidence grow.
– Wife of a traveling businessman

ABOUT THE AUTHOR

Matthew S. McNaughton was born and raised in Fresno, California. He is a life-long member of The Church of Jesus Christ of Latter-day Saints. Born the last of six children, he was taught and tutored by loving parents and supportive siblings. At the age of seventeen, Brother McNaughton's testimony took a giant leap forward. While working in the backyard with his father, a massive heart attack took the life of the man he so dearly loved and admired. His grief was incomparable. A spiritual experience following the passing of his father would change his life forever.

Over the past twenty-two years, Brother McNaughton has spent countless nights away from his loved ones. Due to his profession, he has logged hundreds of thousands of miles in the air and countless nights in hotels. Though he yearned to be home with his wife and children, traveling became a way of life. For some, a life style filled with a myriad of opportunities to succumb to the temptations of Satan.

Following Brother McNaughton's mission to Louisiana, he married his college sweetheart; Kathy Louise Pelton. He has served in many church positions; taught seminary, elders quorum president, high council, high priest group leader, stake presidency and currently serving as the stake young men's president. By profession, he is the director of sales for a major beauty care company. Brother McNaughton lives in Puyallup, Washington with his wife and six children.

Contents

ACKNOWLEDGMENTS vii

ABOUT THE AUTHOR xi

CHAPTER ONE
LISTENING EARS 1

CHAPTER TWO
ARMOR OF GOD 17

CHAPTER THREE
WITHIN THESE WALLS 31

CHAPTER FOUR
OPPOSITES MUSTN'T ATTRACT 55

CHAPTER FIVE
SHAPE UP.. 69

CHAPTER SIX
FIRST THINGS FIRST 87

CHAPTER SEVEN
TRAVEL WITH YOUR TESTIMONY ... 99

CHAPTER EIGHT
HONEST IN YOUR DEALINGS 109

CHAPTER NINE
FINAL APPROACH 119

EPILOGUE 125

Jesus, Savior, Pilot Me

Jesus, Savior, pilot me over life's tempestuous sea; Unknown waves before me roll, hiding rock and treacherous shoal. Chart and compass came from thee: Jesus, Savior, pilot me.

As a mother stills her child, Thou canst hush the ocean wild; Boisterous waves obey thy will, when thou say'st to them, "Be still!"
Wondrous Sovereign of the sea,
Jesus, Savior, pilot me.

When at last I near the shore, and the fearful breakers roar, Twixt me and the peaceful rest, Then, while leaning on thy breast, May I hear thee say to me, "Fear not: I will pilot thee."

Text: Edward Hopper

Chapter One
LISTENING EARS

On a cold winter morning in 1997, I found myself sitting in the Seattle airport waiting for yet another flight. On this day my travels would take me to Anchorage, Alaska. Having been raised in California, I became somewhat accustomed to warm weather. Alaska was not a place I desired to be during the winter. As the plane was making its final approach into Anchorage, I noticed a dark fog that seemed to envelop the entire city. For the next five days, I would endure some of the coldest and dreariest weather I have ever experienced.

Arriving several hours prior to my first appointment, I had the opportunity to do a little sightseeing. Due to the weather, tourism was not the popular event of the day. Prior to my trip, I had heard about a special monument in the downtown area of Anchorage that was worth visiting. I was looking for a statue of a dog that in some way represented something special to the people of Alaska. After walking a few blocks, I came upon the statue. With my limited knowledge of dog breeds, I determined it was a replica of a Siberian husky.

I took out my camera and snapped a photo. After viewing the sculpture for a moment, my eyes glanced down to a postcard that was resting on the monument. I picked up the card and read the following:

Matthew S. McNaughton

"Dedicated to the indomitable spirit of the sled dog that relayed antitoxin six hundred miles over rough ice, across treacherous waters, through arctiblizzards from Nenana to the relief of a stricken Nome in the winter of 1925."

ENDURANCE - FIDELITY – INTELLIGENCE

As I walked away from that monument, I was left with many questions regarding that heroic event. I was utterly intrigued. I read books, viewed videos and asked many questions. I learned all I could about the events surrounding the diphtheria outbreak in Nome, Alaska, during the winter of 1925.

On January 20, 1925, a radio signal went out, flashing for miles across the frozen tundra:

Nome calling.... Nome calling.... We have an outbreak of diphtheria.... No serum.... Urgently need help....

Diphtheria is an extremely contagious disease affecting the throat and lungs. If not treated properly and quickly, it can reach epidemic proportions. The frantic search for antitoxin began.

Seattle calling.... Seattle calling.... Fresh serum available here.... Airplanes standing by to fly to Nome....

Heavy snow and frigid temperatures engulfed the western portion of Alaska. Weather conditions were beyond the technical capabilities of early airplanes with open cockpits.

Anchorage calling.... Anchorage calling.... Ample supply of serum located in hospital here.... Package can be shipped by train to Nenana.... Package weighs 20 pounds.... Could serum be carried to Nome on Iditarod trail by mail drivers and dog teams?

The following day, three children in Nome had died of the deadly disease and more cases had been diagnosed. Time would be the difference between life and death. A relay of dog teams along the Iditarod Trail was quickly organized.

Seven days following the initial cry for help, the serum arrived in Nenana by train. The relay to the stricken city began. Through blinding snow and hurricane-force winds, the desperately needed serum was passed from dog team to dog team. Before daybreak on February 2, 1925, the serum finally arrived in Nome. The 674-mile trip was completed in 127.5 hours. History was made, and the town was saved!

Each year during the first week in March, the Iditarod Sled Dog Race is held to commemorate the historic serum run of 1925. From Anchorage, in South Central Alaska, to Nome, on the Western Bering Sea coast, each team of twelve to eighteen dogs and their musher cover 1,100 miles within nine days to three weeks. It has been called the "Last Great Race on Earth" and has won worldwide acclaim.

As I continued to study about this awe-inspiring event, my admiration and respect for the sled dog grew. I developed a sincere love for these animals and desired to own one. After a couple months of searching, I purchased two Siberian huskies and a training cart made for the road.

Matthew S. McNaughton

My wife figured I was going through a mid-life crisis or had just totally lost my mind. Perhaps a combination of the two. Why would a man in his forties, consumed with the responsibilities of family, church and profession, desire such a thing? She couldn't understand my insatiable desire to have my own little dog sled team. Realizing the anomaly of my newly discovered hobby, and much to the chagrin of my children, I was determined to run my little team through the streets of Puyallup, Washington. After a few months of tedious training and conditioning, we were ready for the road.

The most crucial element in running a team of dogs is the communication between the musher and the lead dog. Unlike a team of horses, there are no reigns or devices for steering. The direction in which the dogs travel is based upon the lead dogs ability to listen to the voice of the musher and follow his commands. The dogs are trained at an early age to listen, learn and follow the commands of their master. A clear line of communication must be accessible at all times. A myriad of distractions can and will occur during any given run. If the dogs fail to listen to the Master's commands and succumb to the distractions and diversions surrounding them, disaster will surely follow.

I would love to report that my first experience running my little dogsled was a success. To my dismay, it was one calamity after another. The few months of training in a vacant field did not properly prepare my team for the busy streets of Puyallup.

At the beginning of the run, the dogs looked beautiful, with their tails standing high and their tongues hanging to the side of their open mouths. They were pulling hard, and I was having the ride of my life. I was so proud of my little team. Just as contentment set in, disaster struck. An elderly couple was walking their little dog on the other side of the road. My two Siberian huskies, (Thunder and Sitka) decided to pay the elderly couple and their little dog a visit. The dogs pulled abruptly to the left and sprinted toward their target. I screamed out, "gee, gee." Gee is the word used to instruct the dogs to turn right. My commands did no good, as the dogs were totally consumed by the distraction. I was both angry and embarrassed. I had to dismount my cart and physically contain my dogs. I couldn't understand why my dogs were so disobedient after three months of perfect behavior. I soon realized that it had nothing do to with their behavior; it had to do with their inability to hear my voice and obey my commands.

As children of a loving Heavenly Father, we, too, need to listen, learn and follow the commands of our Master. God our Father speaks to us and gives us guidance and direction through the Holy Ghost. He will never force us to turn in any specific direction. We are free to choose. However, if we fail to listen and follow the commands of our Master, we, too, will succumb to the distractions and diversions of the Adversary.

Listening ears, coupled with an understanding mind and faithful heart, are the key elements needed in hearing the voice of the Lord. The Lord has informed us more than once of the need to hear His voice.

> Hearken, O ye people of my church, saith the voice of him who dwells on high, and whose eyes are upon all men; yea, verily I say: Hearken ye people from afar; and ye that are upon the islands of the sea, listen together.

> For verily the voice of the Lord is unto all men, and there is none to escape; and there is no eye that shall not see, neither ear that shall not hear, neither heart that shall not be penetrated.
>
> And the rebellious shall be pierced with much sorrow; for their iniquities shall be spoken upon the housetops, and their secret acts shall be revealed. And the voice of warning shall be unto all people, by the mouths of my disciples, whom I have chosen in these last days. (D&C 1:1–4)

The greatest disaster that we could ever experience in this life is to be disconnected from the Savior.

> And the arm of the Lord shall be revealed; and the day cometh that they who will not hear the voice of the Lord, neither the voice of his servants, neither give heed to the words of the prophets and apostles, shall be cut off from among the people. (D&C 1:14)

The "cutting off" process occurs when we turn our listening ears away from the Lord. One of the Savior's greatest responsibilities and desires is to guide our lives. He wants us to listen to His voice and follow His commands. He knows the troubles and tribulations that await us if we don't. He will not forcibly steer us in the right direction. He will whisper quietly the truths we need to hear. The problem is, we fail to hear most of what He says. And when we do hear what He says, we sometimes fail to give heed to His counsel.

Having listening ears and learning to give heed to what we hear, requires the application of four basic principles.

1. Prayer.

Communication with Heavenly Father is the most important and fundamental of all the principles. We must develop our own private and personal relationship with the Lord. Family prayer and personal prayer alone will not suffice. We need to develop a passion within our soul to call on His name many times throughout the day. Whether we pour out our heart in earnest prayer or a simple "Father, I love thee," Prayer will draw us close to the Lord and allow us to be guided by the Holy Ghost through our listening ears.

Each day as we leave our homes and depart into the world, we literately go to battle with the Adversary. The greatest battles we will ever experience in this life will be found within our own soul. I liken our battles unto those of David. Like David, we, too, can be saved from the personal battles that wage against us.

> As for me, I will call upon God; and the Lord shall save me. Evening and morning, and at noon, will I pray, and cry aloud: and he shall hear my voice. And he hath delivered my soul in peace from the battle that was against me: for there were many with me. (Psalm 55: 16–18)

During a recent Sacrament Service, I found myself drifting away into another world. I was not listening to the speaker. Instead, I was having my own private pity party as I was contemplating my travels for the coming week. Another five days and four nights away from my wife and children. The thought of leaving my loved ones created resentment within my heart. To make things worse, I caught wind of what was being spoken at the pulpit. The speaker was talking about the importance of holding family prayer and companion prayer on a daily basis. Knowing that this would be highly impossible for someone who travels, I continued to lament over the matter.

As the closing hymn was being sung, I humbled myself to the point where the Spirit whispered some very important truths. I learned through the Spirit that I never had to miss another family or companion prayer. I visualized myself kneeling down in my hotel room, with telephone in hand, praying together with my loving wife. Though we would be miles apart, we would be joined together in humble prayer to our Heavenly Father. I also visualized leading my family in prayer through the use of a speakerphone. My personal revelation overwhelmed my heart. My pity party suddenly turned into a moment of rejoicing. I realized that I never had to miss another family prayer or companion prayer.

President Romney said, "Pray. Pray diligently. Pray with each other. Pray in public in the proper places. Learn to talk to the Lord; call upon his name in great faith and confidence."

Through prayer, you can call down the blessings of heaven and experience the gift of the Holy Ghost. Earnest and constant prayer will help you avoid the turbulence of the Adversary, thus allowing you to be guided by His Holy Spirit.

2. Study the Scriptures.

Of all the materials you pack for your business trip, your scriptures are the most important and beneficial. Never leave your home or office without them. Your scriptures will serve as your companion while you're away. While in your hotel room, keep them on the nightstand and read them morning and night. Reading and studying the scriptures each day will quicken your mind, spark your spirit and balance your life. Peace, joy and happiness are the blessings that come from reading and studying the scriptures.

Elder Neal A. Maxwell taught, "The scriptures are doors with immense truths behind them, divine insights of major proportions; there is an eternal curriculum—things God would have all men and women upon the face of the earth learn for their happiness."

We live in a world of unstableness and commotion. The scriptures function as our balancing agent, giving us the steadiness and focus we need for spiritual growth.

Along with the scriptures, develop a habit of taking along other good books to read. Books that will edify, uplift and inspire. Reading the scriptures along with other good books will draw you close to the Lord, thereby giving you the spiritual stability and awareness needed to hear His voice.

And as all have not faith, seek ye diligently and teach one another words of wisdom; yea, seek ye out of the best books words of wisdom, seek learning even by study and also by faith. (D&C 109:7)

3. Righteous Living:

Growing up in an athletic family, I had the opportunity to witness and participate in many sporting events. I'll never forget the lesson my older brother taught me following one of his track meets. As he stood on the victory stand, prepared to receive his gold medal, it was obvious that he was not pleased with his performance. Taking first place and winning the gold was an insignificant tribute— simple remembrance that he was only better than the other participants on that particular day. The gold medal in no way represented the quality of the competition or the effort displayed. Regardless of the accolade, he knew he could do better. He learned not to judge his progress by the number of medals he won or competitors he beat. He never compared himself to others. Win or lose, his greatest satisfaction came when he was able to better his own marks and standards, thereby bringing him closer to his ultimate goal.

Have you ever found yourself comparing your spiritual development to that of others? Unfortunately, this is a common practice for many people in the church. How can one compare their personal relationship with the Savior to those of others? Not only is this impossible but also it is highly unnecessary and inappropriate. Your personal relationship with the Savior is personal. Things of a personal nature are guarded, protected, private and special.

Following a recent stake conference, my wife appeared somewhat melancholy during our drive home. In questioning her about her apparent disposition, she calmly said; "Sister Smith is so spiritual, she has it all together." The conversation came to a stop, but I'm sure my wife's next sentence was going to be, "I need to be more like Sister Smith." My wife didn't know Sister Smith or her current circumstances. She has no idea what Sister Smith goes through on a daily basis. It was highly unfair for my dear wife to place unnecessary and unrealistic pressure on herself. The basis for her synopsis was due to the way Sister Smith and her children dressed and sat calmly throughout the duration of stake conference. Yes, from the outside, the Smiths are indeed a model family. However, the outside is insignificant to the Lord. It's what's inside that matters. During the Sermon on the Mount, the Lord said:

> "Blessed are the pure in heart, for they shall see God." (Matthew 5:8)

Our ultimate goal is to live a life of righteousness, so one day we can return and see God our Father and His son Jesus Christ. Righteous living is performed from the inside out. The Psalmist asked,

> "Who shall ascend into the hill of the Lord? or who shall stand in his holy place? He that hath clean hands, and a pure heart; who hath not lifted up his soul unto vanity, nor sworn deceitfully." (Psalms 24:3–4)

Alma taught,

> "I say unto you, can ye look up to God at that day with a pure heart and clean hands? I say unto you, can you look up, having the image of God engraven upon your countenances?" (Alma 5:19)

To have a pure heart, one must refrain from forbidden desires. To have clean hands, we must involve ourselves with acts of righteousness and refrain from acts of wickedness.

It's difficult to live a righteous life all the time. We are all imperfect beings and fall short from time to time. For some, falling short is amplified while traveling away from home on business or other occasions. I've seen many good men and women lower their standards to accommodate their social environment. Righteous living is not based on where you are at the moment. Righteous living is a constant behavior. Regardless of the company, our standards should never change.

Subsequent chapters will reinforce the importance of living a righteous life while away from home. Many examples, ideas and experiences will be shared to spread light and knowledge on this subject. Each time you leave your home to embark on yet another business trip, make this pledge to yourself; "I promise this day, to return home with clean hands and a pure heart."

4. Service.

Throughout my life, some of my greatest spiritual experiences occurred while I was in the service of my fellow men. I was taught as a young boy the importance of this great principle.

Once a month, my father would pick me up during my lunch hour at school to home teach a less active family. Not only was this family less active, but also they were considered "no contacts." Because we were not welcome in their home, we would visit the Priesthood holder at his place of business. Since he worked at a gas station, my father always made sure his gas tank was on "empty" for this special day. I remember having negative feelings toward my father for taking me away from my friends to visit some old guy at a gas station. I may never know the long-term effects that our visits had on this brother, but I will never forget the feelings I felt for serving my fellow man. I didn't realize at that time the multitude of hidden blessings that would come from doing the Lord's work.

Service is essential to be a true follower of Christ. Whether our service is to our fellowmen, or to God, it is the same. As King Benjamin taught his followers, "When ye are in the service of your fellow beings ye are only in the service of your God" (Mosiah 2:17). One of the most affectionate ways we can show our love for the Savior is to feed his sheep.

Through modern revelation the Lord has commanded us to "succor the weak, lift up the hands which hang down, and strengthen the feeble knees" (D&C 81:5). In a recent family prayer, my fourteen-year-old daughter Katie prayed for Heavenly Father to bless the sick, the poor and the needy. Following her prayer, I asked her how Heavenly Father was going to accomplish this. She responded by saying, "Heavenly Father can do anything."

Several years ago while attending a divisional sales meeting, the president of the company shared the following story.

"There was once a man who inherited a large piece of land. The land was covered with trees, rocks and sagebrush. Over the years, people used the land to dump trash and other forms of debris. The piece of land was an eyesore to all who looked upon it. The man labored hard for four years to clean up his property and to develop his land into a place of beauty. He built a lovely home in the midst of the property. Surrounding his home was a beautiful pond with elegant landscaping.

"One day the local preacher came by to visit the man. Prior to inviting the preacher into his home, the man gave the preacher a tour of his property. After the tour was complete, the preacher looked at the man and said, 'God has richly blessed you with a beautiful home, a lovely pond and a gorgeous piece of property. He sure has created a lovely earth hasn't he? Isn't God magnificent?' The man, somewhat perplexed, said, 'You think this is the work of God? You should have seen this property when God owned it by himself!'"

Heavenly Father does not magically reach out and make bad things good and difficult things easy. He has instructed us to be "anxiously engaged in a good cause, and to do many things of our own free will, and to bring to pass much righteousness" (D&C 58:27).

As followers of Christ, we have all made a covenant to bless our fellowman. We are the tools that God utilizes to bless his children. We do this through priesthood blessings, acts of service and gifts of love. Our acts and gifts must be motivated by charity, which is the pure love of Christ.

Throughout my life, I have always felt the most guidance when I was doing God's work, whether fulfilling my church calling or providing service for one of his children. Alma, teaching the words of Abinadi, said:

Behold, here are the waters of Mormon (for thus they were called) and now, as ye are desirous to come into the fold of God, and to be called his people, and are willing to bear one another's burdens, that they may be light;

Yea, and are willing to mourn with those that mourn; yea, and comfort those that stand in need of comfort, and to stand as witnesses of God at all times and in all things, and in all places that ye may be in, even until death, that ye may be redeemed of God, and be numbered with those of the first resurrection, that ye may have eternal life.

Now I say unto you, if this be the desire of your heart, what have you against being baptized in the name of the Lord, as a witness before him that ye have entered into a covenant with him, that ye will serve him and keep his commandments, that he may pour out his Spirit more abundantly upon you? (Mosiah 18:8–10)

Baptized members of the Church have taken upon themselves several covenants. One in particular is to serve the Lord and keep his commandments. By doing so, the Lord will bless us with his Spirit.

By living according to these four principles, Prayer, Scripture Study, Righteous Living and Service, we will develop a relationship with the Savior that will allow us to feel His Spirit at all times and in all places. We will then be blessed with the ability to give heed to His council through our listening ears.

Chapter Two
ARMOR OF GOD

As a young boy, I had a deep passion for athletics, football being my favorite. I think I enjoyed wearing the uniform as much as I did playing the game. My armor gave me confidence and made me feel invincible. I considered myself a warrior preparing for battle. Except for my arms and lower legs, all parts of my body were protected. With the help of my uniform, my body could sustain a blow of considerable force.

Prior to each football game, I carefully applied each part of my armor to my body. I always took a little extra time when placing my pads within my pants. There are separate compartments in the pant for the kneepads and thigh pads. The hip pads and a tail pad are placed within a girdle that is worn underneath the pant. Each protective device serves a purpose. The pads do not prevent contact; they simply protect the body when contact is made.

Prior to one particular game, I forgot to insert my tail pad. I didn't notice it until the bus was at the stadium. I didn't worry too much about it, due to the fact that the tail pad is so small and seemed so insignificant. What would be the odds of injuring my tailbone? Once the game began, I forgot about the absence of my tail pad—that is to say until the fourth quarter. I'll never forget that play.

Matthew S. McNaughton

It was third down and twenty yards to go for a first down. As a linebacker, my responsibility was to contain the middle and watch for the screen pass. However, the defensive coach called for a blitz.

To this day I'll never forget that call, "Red Dog, Red Dog"; the two linebackers were to blitz right up the middle. The quarterback dropped back and the offensive line set up in a pass block formation. I stormed up the middle with the intensity of a raging bull. Just as I got my hands on the quarterback, a little runningback blocked me below my knees. I did a complete summersault and landed right on my tailbone. I tried to get up but the pain was too intense. With assistance from my teammates, I finally made it to the sidelines. I couldn't sit and could hardly walk. It was soon determined that I broke my tailbone. For months, I would feel the pains of my mistake. If only I had remembered to put on my entire armor, I probably wouldn't have had such an uncomfortable experience.

Each day as we depart our homes, we enter the playing field. The opposition is determined to hit us and injure us if possible. If Satan can take us out of the game and place us on the injured reserve list, he claims victory. He will hit us from every angle. He will concentrate his blows where we are most vulnerable.

We are taught in the scriptures that only God knows our thoughts and the intents of our heart (D&C 6:16). However, Satan knows our habits and will take advantage of any given situation.

Through my experiences, I have learned that I have many weaknesses. Some weaknesses are greater than others. After recovering from my broken tailbone, I was fitted with a special tail pad. An extra thick pad was created to protect my area of weakness. I knew that this area was extremely vulnerable and the possibility of re-injuring my tailbone was likely.

We must be cognizant of our weaknesses. We all have them. Satan will work on our greatest weakness first. Once he feels that we have succumbed to his enticing, he will then move on to our next weakness. The objective is to not succumb to Satan's temptations. We are taught that the Savior suffered temptation but gave no heed unto them (D&C 20:22). We, too, must learn how to suffer temptation without giving heed.

AVOID THE APPEARANCE OF EVIL

Make a habit each day to wrap an extra-thick pad around your weakness. Whatever it might be, we have the means and power to protect ourselves from the blows of the Adversary. The single greatest way to accomplish this is to avoid any area that might resemble trouble.

While serving in a stake presidency, I had a young man come in for a temple recommend interview. During the interview, it was discovered that the young father was experiencing some trouble with the Law of Chastity. Because his travels took him away from home each week, he began to experience inappropriate passions. He informed me that Satan has tempted him with pornography. I then asked the young father if he could determine when this temptation seemed to escalate. He responded; "Every time I enter a convenience store and glance at the magazine rack." My counsel was short and direct: "Stay out of those convenience stores."

In my many interviews and conversations, I have discovered that the vast majority of people place themselves in situations where they allow the Adversary to gradually grind away at their armor. Little by little, their spiritual immune system begins to weaken. If not properly treated, it will only be a matter of time before Satan can break through the armor and create havoc in our lives. You must be wise and watch for the warning signs. When the warning signs come, you need to condition yourself to quickly turn the other way and run. To illustrate this principle, let me share with you the following experience:

Several years ago, I was traveling on business in the Monterey Bay area of California. Because of the distance from my home, it became necessary to stay a few evenings in a hotel. Since I had nothing planned for the evenings, I decided to work as late as possible, in hopes of returning home a day early. It was about 7:00 pm when I came in contact with a young lady who worked at the same store I was servicing. I could tell from her questions that she was interested in more than just casual conversation. I felt uncomfortable and made the decision to call it a day and return to my hotel. I politely excused myself and made my way to the car.

The hotel in which I was staying was only a few blocks away. I checked into the hotel and found my way to the room, which was located on the first floor. Within a very short period of time, a knock came at my door. I looked through the peephole and noticed that it was the same young lady who I met a few hours earlier. What did she want? Why was she at my door? How did she know where I was staying? I didn't stick around to find out, as I quickly made a dash for the back sliding glass door. I jumped into my car and drove towards Carmel. After a few hours of driving around, I came back to the hotel, grabbed my bags and checked out.

In sharing this story with a few close friends, they laughed at me and considered my behavior a lack of strength and courage. I don't know about their synopsis, but I do know that I returned home at the end of that week clean and pure.

On another occasion, I was flying from Seattle to New York. As the aircraft was beginning to land, I was staring out the left window at the runway below. To relieve tension caused by the flight, I usually play a silly little timing game with the actual landing of the aircraft. At a certain point, I start to count down from fifty and see if I can time my countdown with the actual landing. As my countdown reached three, the aircraft suddenly accelerated and shot straight up in the air. Many of the passengers screamed and some began to cry. Once the plane reached a safe altitude, the pilot informed the crew and passengers that there was an unidentified aircraft sitting in the middle of the runway. To avoid tragedy, the pilots only choice was to make a radical move away from the danger lurking below. Because of the pilot's actions, many lives were saved that day.

I've always been taught to never run away from my problems. This is true in the case of ongoing personal trials but not in the case of a sudden spiritual emergency. If you ever see, feel, or sense any turbulence caused by the Adversary, emulate the pilot and make a radical move away from the potential danger.

To put on the full armor of God means to envelop oneself with righteousness. By wrapping yourself in righteousness, you protect yourself from the fiery darts of Satan. You can't stop the darts, but you can shield yourself from their evil infiltration. This principle is clearly taught in the Doctrine and Covenants.

> Wherefore, lift up your hearts and rejoice, and gird up your loins, and take upon you my whole armor, that ye may be able to withstand the evil day, having done all that ye may be able to stand.
>
> Stand, therefore, having your loins girt about with truth, having on the breastplate of righteousness, and your feet shod with the preparation of the gospel of peace, which I have sent mine angels to commit unto you.
>
> Taking the shield of faith wherewith ye shall be able to quench all the fiery darts of the wicked;
>
> And take the helmet of salvation, and the sword of my spirit, which I will pour out upon you, and my word which I reveal unto you, and be agreed as touching all things whatsoever ye ask of me, and be faithful until I come, and ye shall be caught up, that where I am ye shall be also. (D&C 27:15–18)

AS A MAN THINKETH

The next step is to reprogram your thought process. The Savior said: "As a man thinketh, so is he." So what are you thinking? What occupies your mind? Before we do anything of a physical nature, we always think it through in our mind first. Each one of us is personally responsible for what we do. When questioning my children about a bonehead mistake they made, I often get the response, "I'm sorry, Dad. I guess I just wasn't thinking." Wrong! Not only were they thinking, but they carefully planned it out. Our thoughts always precede our actions.

So how do we go about reprogramming our thoughts? First, we must understand that our thoughts are not private. We might be able to hide our thoughts from our spouse, friends, boss and bishop, but we can't hide our thoughts from God. He knows our thoughts and the intents of our heart. This knowledge should be motivation enough to alter our thoughts. Unfortunately, our minds have the ability to record polluted events that are seen by our eyes and heard by our ears. At any given time, our mind can recall such events. This is why we struggle from time to time with our thoughts. We are instructed to let virtue garnish our thoughts.

> Let virtue garnish thy thoughts unceasingly; then shall thy confidence wax strong in the presence of God; and the doctrine of the priesthood shall distil upon thy soul as the dews from heaven. (D&C 121:45)

To cultivate wholesome thoughts, we must plant seeds of righteousness in our minds. The best time to plant seeds of righteousness is in the early hours of the morning. Develop a habit each morning to study the scriptures and go to your Heavenly Father in earnest prayer. Ask Heavenly Father to bless you with positive and wholesome thoughts. As you get up from your knees and depart into the world, be aware of the Adversary and his evil tactics.

One of Satan's many tools is the radio. This holds true especially for the professional who travels the road. The airwaves are contaminated with filthy music, disc jockeys, hosts and guests. Some people find them interesting, entertaining and titillating. Don't allow yourself to be subjected to such garbage. Preset your stations to wholesome and uplifting music or talk radio. If you come across an inappropriate station, change that station as fast as you can. To help maintain a wholesome and healthy mind, you must refrain from the trash that is so freely poured out over the airwaves.

For ten years I worked as a traveling salesman. I drove between 3,000 and 5,000 miles each month servicing my accounts. I had every opportunity to allow my mind to drift into lustful thoughts. I kept my mind actively engaged in a good cause. The majority of the time I kept my radio silent, as I pondered upon my upcoming sales call or other activities of the day. Thousands of prayers were uttered and most were answered while I was driving from one city to another. It's amazing how clear the still small voice can be when you surround yourself with peace and quiet. When you're ready for some company, listen to motivational tapes, conference tapes or wholesome music. Don't allow the radio to intervene with your desire to have clean and wholesome thoughts.

As traveling professionals, you interface with all types of people with varying standards. You're subjected to profanity, dirty jokes, backbiting and gossip. You see pornography on the walls of offices and warehouses. You receive invitations for after-hours drinks with customers, executives and clients. There are those who attempt to deceive customers and manipulate the system for their gain. You've been in the presence of the dishonest and unfaithful. Perhaps you have encountered advances from the opposite sex. As followers of Christ, we strive to walk in the footsteps of the Savior. However, we still walk side by side with our neighbor. How do we maintain our morals while at the same time being influenced by worldly decay? The following story is a perfect example.

Several years ago I had the opportunity to assist in the planning of an Area Conference. One of my main responsibilities was transporting the Brethren to and from their several meetings and assignments. We were equipped with all the necessities to assure the safety of the Brethren. The one thing I had no control of was the behavior of the people we came in contact with.

After the conference was complete and just prior to the departure of the Brethren back to Salt Lake, I was engaged in a conversation with Elder James E. Faust. As we were talking, a rugged old man approached us and then suddenly turned and walked off. Just as he was leaving, Elder Faust reached out and grabbed the old man's arm. Elder Faust said, "How are you, brother?" The old man then let out a stream of profanity to express his disposition. I was mortified! I felt responsible that an Apostle of the Lord was subjected to such language.

After the man finished expressing his feelings, a marvelous lesson was taught. Elder Faust gently reached out and grabbed the man's arm and said, "God love you, brother." After the man walked off, Elder Faust calmly turned to me and continued our conversation from where we left off. Nothing was said about the incident. Elder Faust was impervious to the explicit language. I'm sure he didn't enjoy hearing such words, but he certainly didn't allow it to stain his spirit.

Don't be so naive as to think that God will protect your ears and eyes from the garbage of the world. We can control what we hear and see in our homes, but not in the world. If we prepare ourselves spiritually each day, we will be able to fend off the evil darts of the Adversary.

The most important element is the understanding that we can govern our thoughts. We can decide what we want to think about. If an inappropriate thought enters your mind, emulate the computer and hit delete. Remove the thought as quickly as possible. Do not allow the thought to ruminate in your mind. As magnificent as the mind is, it's interesting to note that it can only think one thought at a time. As an inappropriate thought enters into your mind, replace it with a clean thought. Capture the unsuitable thought and throw it aside. When I say throw it aside, I'm talking mentally, physically and spiritually. Mentally remove the thought. At times I actually say to myself, "Thought, get out of my mind."

A colleague of mine shared the following example: "Whenever an impure or negative thought enters my mind, I raise both feet off the ground and hold that position until the thought leaves. Without fail, my impure thoughts are replaced with thoughts of physical pain and discomfort." If the thought continues, invite the Spirit to assist you. Sing your favorite hymn, call your spouse, quote a scripture, or ponder your many blessings. We do indeed have the power to control our thoughts.

In referring to the mind, I love the quote by James Allen: "You will become as small as your controlling desire; as great as your dominant aspiration." Aspire to be great and seek to keep your mind clean and your thoughts wholesome.

WEAKNESS AND HUMILITY

Before we can safeguard ourselves from temptation, we must first acknowledge that we have weaknesses. We must then pinpoint which weakness is of greatest concern. We should not feel guilty because of our weaknesses. The Lord gave us weaknesses to teach us humility. Weakness in and of itself is not a sin. It's not until we entertain thoughts of acting upon our weakness and yielding to that weakness that it can become sinful. The Savior said, "As a man thinketh, so is he."

To illustrate this point, let me share a personal weakness of mine. I stated earlier that I love sports. One of the perks I receive with my job is season tickets to professional sporting events. Unfortunately, most football games and many basketball and baseball games are played on Sunday. In my heart, I know that I should not attend any games that are played on the Sabbath. However, I allow my mind to lament over the matter. My mind is trying to convince my heart that my decision to attend a sporting event on the Sabbath could be justified. I hold the tickets delicately in my hands and ponder the possibilities. Do I have any assignments at church today? Would anyone miss me? What can I use as an excuse? What would I tell my wife? I suffer temptation each week, trying to justify my decision to disobey the commandments. Why do I do this? Because I have been given weaknesses.

Some of our weaknesses are more significant than others. Regardless of their magnitude, the Lord promises us that we can turn our weaknesses into strengths.

And if men come unto me I will show them their weakness, I give unto men weakness that they may be humble; and my grace is sufficient for all men that humble themselves before me; for if they humble themselves before me, and have faith in me, then will I make weak things become strong unto them. (Ether 12:27)

According to this scripture, we must apply three principles in overcoming our weaknesses:

1. We must first draw close to the Lord through earnest prayer, scripture study and active involvement in church meetings, service and activities. By doing so, we become more susceptible to the promptings of the Spirit.

2. Once we allow the Savior to direct our lives, we learn how weak we really are without him. Strength comes only through the constant companionship of the Holy Ghost. We learn sincere humility when we come unto the Lord and cast our burdens upon Him.

3. When we truly humble ourselves before the Lord and have faith in Him, blessings of strength, wisdom, grace and mercy will follow. The Lord then promises us that HE will make our weak things become strong.

When temptations and trials come your way, remember the powerful promise of the Savior:

"To him that overcometh will I grant to sit with me in my throne, even as I also overcame, and am set down with my Father in his throne" (Revelations 3:21).

The key word is overcometh,—meaning to overcome trials, tribulations, temptations and weaknesses. The Lord knew we would experience hardships in our lives. Great blessings await us as we overcome our weaknesses and strive to be more like the Savior.

We must be ever vigilant of the Adversary in our day-to-day travels. Pray daily for the Spirit, but beware of Satan's tactics. He's out there lurking around every corner. Don't lower your standards and values just because you're away from home.

While serving as an Elders Quorum President, I had a young man in my quorum who traveled periodically with his job. In confidence, he shared with me some struggles he was experiencing while on the road. He informed me that whenever he was alone in his hotel room, it became easy for him to resort to sexual self-gratification. I asked him what he meant by alone. In response he said, "Alone; you know, by myself." I then asked him if he would feel comfortable doing this act in the presence of his mother, father or wife. He had a look of terror on his face as he exclaimed, "Absolutely not!"

I then asked, "Why then do you feel comfortable doing this in the presence of God?"

He placed his head in his hands and said, "Brother McNaughton, I never considered that."

We must live each minute of our lives with the understanding that God loves us and knows our every thought and act. There is nothing that we do or don't do that God is not aware of. Satan will focus his energies on the weak areas of your armor. You know your weakness. Make sure you "gird up your loins" and wrap yourselves in the whole armor of God. And for those weak areas, make certain you place an extra layer of armor.

Chapter Three
WITHIN THESE WALLS
"The Hotel Room"

Throughout my career I have stayed in hundreds of hotels. From the most expensive and glamorous establishments of the Bahamas and Las Vegas to privately owned motels off Interstate 90. At times I've been treated like royalty and enjoyed the finest of living conditions. I have also experienced the contrary, with motels that had no phones, air conditioning or hot water. Motels that were so unkempt, that I opted to sleep throughout the night in a chair instead of the bed. Hotels or motels, palace or suites, while traveling on business these structures do become your home away from home.

Church leaders have taught that the home and the temple are the only two edifices necessary upon this earth. We can do without many buildings, but we cannot survive spiritually without the home and temple. So where does the hotel fit it? For some, a hotel is synonymous with vacation and pleasure, an escape from the tedious routines of life. For those who travel, it becomes their temporary home and living quarters.

During my twenty-five years of marriage, I have spent over seven years living in hotel rooms. Rooms that have been occupied by thousands before me with various purposes, beliefs and lifestyles.

At the beginning of my career, I found traveling and hotel living to be exciting. I enjoyed the quiet surrounding and found pleasure in room service. I didn't consider the hotel to be my home away from home, I thought of it more like my "dream home away from home." I was so wrapped up in my business and newfound pleasure of traveling; I didn't even feel guilty leaving my young wife and little children at home.

During the summer of 1982, my little "hotel happiness" turned unsightly. Shortly after checking into my room, I felt a distinct distraction. An uncomfortable feeling began to swell within the walls of my hotel room. At first I discounted the feelings as loneliness or boredom. I soon realized that it was something much more severe. I called the front desk and requested to be moved to another room. After learning that the hotel was full, I dropped to my knees and prayed to Heavenly Father. I don't remember my prayer, but I do remember pleading with Heavenly Father to remove the evil spirit that was present. For the first time, I did something that would become a part of my everyday travels. I dedicated my hotel room as a refuge and sanctuary. After my prayer, I immediately felt the comfort of the Spirit. From that day forward, the first item of business I conduct once I enter my hotel room is to drop to my knees and dedicate my room.

On Sunday, March 27, 1836, the Kirtland Temple was dedicated to the Lord. The service began with Signey Rigdon, a councilor in the First Presidency, reading Psalms 96 and 24. He would also offer the invocation and speak for nearly two and a half-hours. Following President Rigdon's remarks, Joseph Smith was sustained as a prophet and seer.

After a few beautiful hymns, Joseph Smith then read the dedicatory prayer, which had been revealed to him. This prayer, recorded in section 109 of the Doctrine and Covenants, contains a petition that the Kirtland Temple "may be a house of prayer, a house of fasting, a house of faith, a house of learning, a house of glory, a house of order, a house of God." The prayer went on to say, "That thy glory may rest down upon thy people, and upon this thy house, which we now dedicate to thee, that it may be sanctified and consecrated to be holy, and that thy holy presence may be continually in this house."

Your hotel room is not a temple, it is not your home, but it is a dwelling for a period of time for your soul. And what can be more important than that? Your hotel room can be your own private house of prayer, house of fasting, house of faith and house of learning. However, if not properly organized and prepared, it can turn into something quite different.

> "For what is a man profited, if he shall gain the whole world, and lose his own soul? or what shall a man give in exchange for his soul?" (Matthew 16:26).

Thousands of righteous souls have been lost within the walls of the hotel room. Each of us has the right to call down the blessings of heaven and dedicate our living space as a refuge and sanctuary from the world. By incorporating this holy practice into your daily travels, you will be comforted, guided and blessed in your daily and nightly activities.

When traveling overnight, remember to bring along a framed photo of your family and a picture of the temple. Place these special emblems on the nightstand next to your bed or in an area where they can be easily seen. Don't ever lose sight of the most precious things in your life. As you focus on your family and the temple, you will lose sight of worldly desires.

PLAN YOUR EVENING ACTIVITIES

In preparing for this section of the book, I interviewed many people (members of the church and non-members) to learn of their evening routines, activities and habits while staying in a hotel. Though their answers varied, they were all consistent with their activities from one evening to the next.

The vast majority of the men and women followed the same schedule. Check in, unpack, change clothes, download email, check voice mail and call home. So far so good. However, from this point on, their schedules begin to change. Some go out for dinner while others order room service. A large percentage of non-members meet up with friends or colleagues for an after-hours drink. A small percentage of the people I interviewed enjoyed an evening run or workout in the gym. A surprisingly large percentage of women make a trip to the local retailer to purchase items they forgot to pack. About 15% use this time for casual reading. Less than 20% complete work related assignments and prepare for the next day's activities. Only 15% of the members of the Church pack their scriptures, and 10% actually read them. An alarming 85% spend the evening hours lying on their beds watching television.

The one element I did find to be consistent with all those I interviewed was the lack of planning out their evening activities.

Having a plan for your evening activities is just as important as having a plan for your daily activities. In fact, the evening plan is much more crucial. Where there is no plan, there is no purpose. Where there is no purpose, there is no desire or goal to achieve righteous results. When we are not moving toward a goal, we are idle in our behavior. We are taught in the Doctrine and Covenants:

> "Cease to be idle; cease to be unclean; cease to find fault one with another; cease to sleep longer than is needful; retire to thy bed early, that your bodies and your minds may be invigorated" (D&C 88:124).

We learn a couple principles from this passage. First, the Lord uses the word cease, which means to stop. Because he is asking us to stop, he is fully aware that we are, or have been, idle in a few or perhaps all of these areas. Sometimes we forget that the Lord doesn't expect us to be perfect. If we begin to fall short of our responsibilities and His expectations of us, the Lord is simply asking us to stop and do better. Secondly, we are taught that our bodies and minds may be invigorated. Isn't this the dream of every human being; to have a strong and healthy mind and body?

I'm a habitual planner. I plan everything I do every day. One Saturday morning, my seventeen-year-old daughter Michelle was reviewing my plans for the day. She laughed out loud as she discovered that I had "shower" listed on my daily plan. She thought it was bizarre that I had to remind myself to take a shower. I informed her that it wasn't written to remind me, it was written to keep my day in order.

The following is my actual evening agenda from my latest road trip. Planning my evenings in this fashion helps keep me organized, focused, busy and worthy while staying in a hotel.

Evening Schedule
Dinner with Doug 6:00 PM
Call home
Download and read email
Complete assignment on fiscal years priorities
Run three miles on tread mill and bike for thirty minutes
Shower
Work on my book
Call Kathy (wife)
Family Prayer with children (over the phone)
Scriptures
Personal Prayer
Bed by 11:30.

As you can see, I have allowed no time for Satan to work on my weaknesses. My plan has a purpose. My purpose has specific goals. I have literally shut the door on Satan's ability to add turbulence to my life.

It doesn't matter how you go about planning your evening activities, it only matters that you do. The average traveler has five hours to deal with at the end of each day. Five hours that can be used productively or wasted on superficial activities. Use this "prime time" to develop spiritually, mentally and physically.

> "Make no little plans;
> they have no magic to stir
> men's blood. And probably
> themselves will not be realized.
> Make big plans; aim high in
> hope and work,
> Remembering that a noble,
> logical diagram once recorded
> will not die."
> —Daniel H. Burnham

HOTEL ROOM HAZARDS

Several years ago, my wife and I took a trip to Louisiana to visit some dear friends from my mission. It was the middle of spring and the South never looked better. My wife learned firsthand the true meaning of "Southern Hospitality." Each day brought a new experience. There would be shrimp and crawfish boils, jambalaya, oysters on the half shell and catfish. We chewed on sarsaparilla root as we toured several beautiful antebellum homes. We visited battlegrounds and cemeteries from the Civil War. We also experienced a "bass boat" ride down a backcountry bayou—an experience my wife will never forget.

The beauty of the bayou was astonishing. Thick green vegetation, colorful flowers and Spanish moss surrounded us. Large willow trees greeted us at every bend. Cranes and various wildlife basked in the noonday sun. We were totally consumed by the beauty of the bayou.

Toward the end of our little journey, we saw a very large willow tree with beautiful moss hanging from its branches. My wife thought it would be the perfect place to stop and snap a picture. As we approached the edge of the river and prepared to step out of the boat, our friends informed us that the river was full of alligators. My wife thought they were kidding as she continued to exit the boat. Having served my mission in Louisiana, I knew that alligators were indigenous to the South. I grabbed my wife's arm and pulled her back into the boat.

Our friends pointed out several alligators calmly lurking in the water below. From our viewpoint, we couldn't see any alligators. What they claimed to be an alligator appeared to be a couple sets of large marbles floating on the surface of the water. They informed us that those marbles are the alligator's watchful eyes. My wife enjoyed the story but was not convinced. She was determined to get a photo of the two of us sitting on that lovely willow tree. The only thing that stood between our perfect photo and the boat was a potential alligator. Because my wife has never occupied the same body of water as an alligator, or experienced an alligator attack, she didn't foresee or understand the possible danger.

As we continued to survey the area, a large gator suddenly jerked in the water and swam away. It was startling, to say the least. Safety became our main priority as we stayed in the boat and encouraged our friends to drive to a safe part of the river.

The bayou, with all its beauty and luster can be a life-savoring experience. It can also be a life-altering experience if caution and a little common sense are not applied. Much like the bayou, your hotel experience can be a night to remember or a dreadful night that you will never forget.

Extreme caution and common sense must be applied while spending a night in a hotel. Most hotels are saturated with hazardous vices, calmly lurking only inches from your soul. These vices have been, and will continue to be, used by Satan to entice and cripple virtually thousands of innocent men and women.

COFFEEMAKER

The National Coffee Association reports that 52% of Americans drink coffee on a daily basis. This equates to 470 million cups of coffee every day. In 2003, over $5 billion dollars of roasted coffee was sold in the United States; it is the second most valuable item of international trade—second only to oil. We are taught in Doctrine and Covenants 89:9

"And again, hot drinks are not for the body or belly."

Church leaders have instructed us that this passage refers to coffee and tea.

One of the first things you see as you enter most hotel rooms is the coffeemaker. Hotels try very hard to make your stay as comfortable and convenient as possible. However, this gratuity is neither comfortable nor convenient if you struggle with the Word of Wisdom. If coffee is one of your weaknesses, this can cause a major problem. Let me recommend a few solutions to remedy this temptation:

> • Search out hotels that do not offer in-room coffeemakers.
> • If you require a hot drink in the morning, bring dry packets of hot chocolate or your own herb tea. The coffeemaker can boil water for hot chocolate or herb tea just as well as it does for coffee.
> • Prior to checking in, request that the coffeemaker be removed from your room. Don't ever feel uncomfortable or embarrassed to request service from the hotel staff.

If you struggle with this portion of the Word of Wisdom, than I suggest you use wisdom and avoid the temptation entirely.

TELEPHONE

There are several people who take credit for the invention of the telephone, however it is Alexander Graham Bell whose name is synonymous with this inspired invention. Bell was born is 1847 in Edinburgh, Scotland. Throughout his life, Bell had been interested in the education of deaf people. This interest motivated him to invent the microphone. Then, in 1876, he invented the "electrical speech machine," which we now call a telephone. By 1878, Bell had set up the first telephone exchange in New Haven, Connecticut. Six years later, long-distance connections were made between Boston and New York City.

I'm sure that Bell imagined great uses for his new invention. Instant oral communication without tangible interaction would be the beginning of a whole new way of life. Unfortunately, this inspired device would also be used for other purposes. Since his death in 1922, the telecommunication industry has undergone an amazing revolution. Bell's "electrical speech machine" paved the way for the Information Superhighway.

Every highway has experienced its fair share of accidents and fatalities. This holds true for the information highway as well. The telephone, if used properly, is a marvelous instrument. If used improperly, the telephone can and will damage your spiritual progress.

During the late 1980s, an evil intruder invaded our phone lines. Phone numbers for accessing pornographic messages and conversations became available. At the time, there was no form of regulation. Men, women and even our precious children spent thousands of hours listening to vulgar dialogue. Over $1 billion per year is spent on what I call "telephone pornography."

In my quest for knowledge and understanding as to why some people invest their time and money into such material; I came up with one motive: boredom. If not curtailed, this type of activity will become an addictive behavior and lead to further involvement in related activities.

"And behold, others he flattereth away, and telleth them there is no hell; and he saith unto them: I am no devil, for there is none—and thus he whispereth in their ears, until he grasps them with his awful chains, from whence there is no deliverance" (2 Nephi 28:22).

Satan will try to convince you that this behavior can be justified. He uses phrases like, "At least you're not committing adultery." This type of justification will allow Satan to grasp you with his awful chains. He's cunning, tricky and evil. He will do whatever he can to destroy your spiritual progress and happiness.

If you properly plan your evening and stay busy, you can avoid any turbulence that Satan might put in your way. Your work will be satisfying and your stay at the hotel will be productive and rewarding.

MINIBAR

Fortunately, minibars are not found in all hotel rooms. Hotels that have them want you to believe that the in-room minibar or refreshment center is there for your convenience. I don't believe sixteen ounces of bottled water selling for $3.00 is a convenience. In-room minibars require significant labor to service, inventory and restock. Minibars in the U.S. have become a break-even, at best, contributor to the hotel's profitability. If minibars were a huge source of revenue, you would see them in all hotels.

Unlike "family" hotel guests, the business traveler is unlikely to bring packaged goods into the room and therefore will vend products if their desired selection is available.

Inner-city hotels and airport hotels in the major business centers of the U.S. find that the average hotel guest does not want to stroll about in search for a beverage or snack outside the hotel and therefore represents a captured audience. The traveling businessperson will utilize the minibar for a beverage or snack approximately 33% of the time.

Most hotels stock their minibars with soft drinks, snacks and alcohol. However, there is a new concept called the "e-fridge minibar system" that is being installed in the four and five-star hotels. Much like your local grocery store, UPC sensor tags are placed under all the products in these new e-fridge systems. When a guest removes an item, a message is relayed to the hotel's property management system. It has been confirmed that replacing the manual minibars with automated minibars will increase revenues by at least 25%. Most of this increase will be due to the elimination of shrinkage and pilferage. As theft from minibars is practically eliminated, more expensive products (film, disposable cameras, cosmetics, fragrance, inappropriate magazines, etc.) will be available to the guest. The hotel minibar is not a convenience; it's a trap! It can be costly; both financially and spiritually.

Several years ago, a friend of mine came to me with a serious problem. He informed me that he was addicted to alcohol and drugs. His addition began as a young boy and continued through his adult life. He married a lovely lady and had six beautiful children. On several different occasions he attempted to rid himself of this terrible disease. He enrolled in rehabilitation institutions, read the scriptures, prayed daily and requested priesthood blessings. His greatest desire was to overcome this weakness and become a worthy husband and father. At one point, he kept himself clean from alcohol and drugs for eighteen months. Obeying the Word of Wisdom brought him and his family an outpouring of blessings.

During one of his business trips, he found himself involved in a personal battle with the minibar. Because of his flight schedule, he didn't have an opportunity to eat dinner. He was hungry and opened the minibar for a light snack to hold him over until breakfast. He grabbed a candy bar and a bag of chips. Before closing the door, his eyes glanced down to a small bottle of vodka. For a quick second, he was tempted to reach for the alcohol. However, he remained strong and left the alcohol behind. As the night grew older, his desire to consume the alcohol became stronger. His battle ended after a few hours of constant torment from the Adversary. That night, he drank every bottle of alcohol that was stocked in the minibar. Unfortunately, that evening would be the beginning of the end for my dear friend. He never recovered from that fall and within a few years he lost his life from the consequences of drugs and alcohol. The Lord said:

> "And all saints who remember to keep and do these sayings, walking in obedience to the commandments, shall receive health in their navel and marrow to their bones; And shall find wisdom and great treasures of knowledge, even hidden treasures; And shall run and not be weary, and shall walk and not faint. And I, the Lord, give unto them a promise, that the destroying angel shall pass by them, as the children of Israel, and shall not slay them. Amen" (D&C 89:18-21).

Upon check-in, you will be handed your room key and the key to the minibar (if available). My simple advice is to take the minibar key and politely hand it back to the clerk. This little act might save you a lot of grief and perhaps even your life. Use wisdom when dealing with in-room minibars.

LAPTOPS / INTERNET

In 1993 I was introduced to my first laptop. During my initial training, a colleague proceeded to teach me how to download email and access the Internet while traveling across the country. He called me over to his side of the desk and proceeded to introduce me to the many wonders of the Internet. Because of my lack of computer knowledge, I was totally consumed with every click of the mouse. Once my initial lesson was complete, he then said, "now let me show you the better things in life." The next few minutes would prove to be one of the most uncomfortable situations I would ever experience. Before I knew it, I was viewing the most degrading material my eyes have ever seen. I was trying to avoid the material while at the same time trying not to offend him.

I soon realized I couldn't do both at the same time. Not being able to find the right words to say, I finally blurted out, "I can't look at those kinds of pictures." He responded by asking, "Why not?" Again, not being able to find the right words, I simply said, "Because I'm not supposed to." He thought my comments were humorous and concluded by saying: "Knowing how much you travel, I thought you might like a little after-hours excitement once in a while." As I contemplate the word excitement, pornography did not make the list of synonyms.

Pornography on the Internet is the fastest-growing virus known to man. Americans are rapidly allowing this evil disease to enter their lives. It's a tragedy that one of the most promising information and communication technologies, the Internet, is being used to satisfy basic human desires.

After excusing an employee from her responsibilities, it became necessary for me to clean up her laptop before issuing it to the next employee. The number of pornographic sites she visited appalled me. Her hard drive was literally saturated with inappropriate material. I was heartbroken and bewildered. Her outward appearance and behavior would never lead one to believe that she would be involved in such activities.

Through my research, I have identified three reasons why the traveling professionals subject themselves to pornographic material.

1. Curiosity. By nature, human beings are curious. We like to know what goes on around us and why. Have you ever come upon a traffic accident and looked away from the incident? Most traffic jams are not necessarily caused by the accident, but rather by curious people slowing down to view the situation.

2. Boredom. We have nothing planned for the evening and become restless and bored. Since our thoughts precede our actions, it's important that we keep our minds actively engaged in worthwhile thoughts. If we don't input wholesome thoughts in our minds, Satan will find a way to clog out minds with negative and other inappropriate thoughts. If you allow the Adversary into your heart, he will convince your mind that this kind of material is interesting, exciting and gratifying.

3. Self-gratification. Millions of people are addicted to pornographic material and use the Internet to satisfy their sexual needs. Pornography for some has become an alternative sexual lifestyle. They feel justified because they are not physically committing adultery or subjecting themselves to sexually transmitted diseases.

> "And verily I say unto you, as I have said before, he that looketh on a woman to lust after her, or if any shall commit adultery in their hearts, they shall not have the Spirit, but shall deny the faith and shall fear." (D&C 63:16)

There's no harm in admiring or even finding someone of the opposite sex attractive; however, we are commanded not to lust after these individuals. Viewing pornographic material will stimulate a massive intrusion of lust in the hearts of men and women. This intrusion of lust will chase away the Spirit and lead to moral decay.

Pornography can be classified as any audio or visual material that causes sexual thoughts or desires. We commit adultery in our heart when we lust after individuals in a sexual way. The Internet has literally millions of links to pornographic sites. As traveling professionals, we must discipline our behavior and never use our laptop for viewing such material. No one will ever force you to view pornographic sites. You are the one who decides where the Web will take you.

"Destiny is not a matter of chance, it is a matter of choice."

The technological advancements of the computer and Internet have been inspired for the advancement of the Gospel of Jesus Christ, not for Satan's utilization. However, Satan has been successful in finding ways to use these inspired innovations for his work. Every time you click on a pornographic site, you become an instrument in furthering Satan's work and thereby fight against the righteous purposes of the Lord.

> "Wherefore, he that fighteth against Zion, both Jew and Gentile, both bond and free, both male and female, shall perish; for they are they who are the whore of all the earth; for they who are not for me are against me, saith our God" (2 Nephi 10:16).

The laptop has become a way of life for the traveler. Countless hours are spent responding to email and completing assignments. The laptop has made traveling more convenient and productive. You can leave your offices and homes without missing important information or due dates. You couldn't be competitive in this ever-changing world of ours without the laptop. Be grateful for modern technology and continue to educate yourself and enhance your skills. If you use your laptop for unrighteous causes, you are literally fighting against Zion and God's holy work. If you use your laptop for righteous endeavors, you will be blessed in your professional life as well as your personal life.

TELEVISION / PAY-PER-VIEW MOVIES

While working as a traveling salesmen, I had the opportunity from time to time to take my children on the road with me. This would always prove to be a learning experience for both of us. On one occasion, my fourteen-year-old son wanted to watch a pay-per-view movie. The movie was rated PG, and I felt it would be appropriate.

However, when I informed my son that we could not view the movie in the hotel room, he became somewhat confused. He stated, "Why not, Dad? It's only $9.95, and we would pay more than that if we went to the theatre." I informed him that it wasn't about money; it was about character and principle.

When hotels first introduced pay-per-view movies, the titles of each movie were listed on the hotel receipt. If a guest had a desire to view an indecent movie, they would think twice before ordering. Realizing that several people could view their receipt, i.e., hotel clerk, spouse and boss, many people decided against viewing inappropriate movies. After a few years of sluggish revenue, movie titles were removed from the hotel receipt. Once this was done, profits went through the roof. The hotel industry claims they made this adjustment to protect your privacy. This is as false a statement as I have ever heard! The decision to remove titles from the hotel receipt was solely based upon money. Though the titles have been removed, code numbers still remain. Don't be foolish to think that your privacy is intact. The movies you watch might be disguised from your spouse or boss but not the hotel, and certainly not Heavenly Father.

I explained to my young son that 80% of all the movies purchased in the hotel room are pornographic in nature. I informed him that I would never want someone to think that I watched an impure movie. Because the titles are not listed, one might surmise that a pornographic movie was purchased. We have been instructed to avoid even the appearance of evil. Though my son's desire to view his PG movie remained, he did understand my logic. Viewing of pornographic movies will warp your mind and spirit quicker than any other material. All pornography is lethal, however movies and videos are the most fatal.

You don't need to purchase a pay-per-view movie to fall prey to pornographic material. Most hotels offer satellite television. As the evening grows old, many networks carry sexually explicit programs. If you want to watch television, research the programs in advance and write down the channel and time of your program. If you channel surf, sooner or later you will land on an inappropriate program. Be careful and use good judgment. Avoiding the television entirely is the only way to guarantee that you will not be subjected to pornographic programming.

If you have a propensity to view inappropriate movies, call the front desk and request that the adult movies in your room are turned off. You can also request this at the time of check in. In many hotels, this procedure can be done from the remote control. To avoid any temptation this might bring, I highly recommend that you request these channels to be turned off at the time you check in.

Satan is patient when it comes to destroying your eternal progress. He likes to work in stages. Of all of Satan's desires, he wants you to be immoral. He wants you to break the Law of Chastity and feel worthless in the eyes of God. He continues to use a systematic plan to capture thousands of worthy men and women. He will tailor his evil plan to suit your weakness. History has taught us that individuals who meddle with pornography will sooner or later experience the following stages.

STAGES OF IMMORALITY

1. Impure thoughts

2. Exposure to pornography
3. Masturbation
4. Affinity toward pornography
5. Addiction to pornography
6. Becoming callous toward things of a spiritual nature
7. Withdrawal from spouse, friends, family and church
8. Acts of Fornication or adultery
9. Separation from spouse, friends, family and church
10. Confusion, discouragement and loss of hope

Though pornography is more prevalent with men, the curiosity and opportunity still exists with women. Pornography does not discriminate. It welcomes everyone to explore its many facets. Don't ever think that you can view such material without it affecting your mind and spirit. It can't be done.

Individuals who view pornographic material are literally clogging and confusing their sexual senses. Pornography desensitizes the pure nature of wholesome intimacy between husbands and wives. Subjecting yourself to pornography has the same effect on the senses as drugs and alcohol. Both vices have a way of confusing the mind and body causing unnatural and immoral feelings of euphoria.

The pornography industry wants to be known as "Adult Entertainment." It tries to create an atmosphere of enjoyment and relaxation. As dangerous as pornography is, there are no warning signs or cautions alerting the prospective consumer of its danger. A simple disclaimer stating that you must be over 18 years of age to purchase is the only stipulation.

Encouraged by the liberal atmosphere of the nineties, adult entertainment in the US has grown into a $12 billion-a-year business. Americans spend more on pornography than they do at cinemas. This epidemic is spreading across the world and affecting the core of the family. Respectable companies such as AT&T with its telephone sex lines; Time Warner, which shows hard-core pornography on its cable networks; and hotel chains with their pay-per-view films have been lured into this despicable business.

We may not be able to remove pornography from the world, but we can eliminate it from our personal lives. If you struggle with pornography, you are not alone. Unlike an incurable cancer, this disease can be cured. It takes understanding, willpower, determination, caution, common sense, personal prayer, daily scripture study and repentance to flush this tendency out of your system. Thousands of men and women have rediscovered sexual purity and wholesome relationships with their spouse. Pure joy and eternal happiness are the blessings that come to those who keep themselves morally clean.

> And moreover, I would desire that ye should consider on the blessed and happy state of those that keep the commandments of God. For behold, they are blessed in all things, both temporal and spiritual; and if they hold out faithful to the end they are received into heaven, that thereby they may dwell with God in a state of never-ending happiness. O remember, remember that these things are true; for the Lord God hath spoken it. (Mosiah 2:41)

By planning properly and avoiding the hazards of the hotel, you're traveling experiences can be delightful and rewarding. You will be blessed in your labors and find joy in your work. No greater joy and satisfaction can be experienced, than by doing what is right in the midst of temptation.

> "There's no thrill in easy sailing
> when the skies are clear and blue,
> there's no joy in merely doing things
> which any one can do.
>
> But there is some satisfaction that
> is mighty sweet to take, when you
> reach a destination that you thought
> you'd never make."
> –Spirella

Chapter Four
OPPOSITES *MUSTN'T* ATTRACT
"For the Married Professional"

When it comes to flying on airplanes, I'm not very good at making small talk. I like my space and prefer to sit alone if at all possible. As the passengers are boarding the plane, I'm the one who buries himself in his paperwork and tries not to make eye contact. I don't mean to be rude or antisocial, I just see this time as an opportunity to catch up on paperwork and other job-related duties.

On a recent flight from Cleveland to Salt Lake, I found myself sitting next to two very attractive women. One appeared to be in her late twenties and the other was in her mid to late forties. As I reached for my briefcase to break out my usual paperwork, the younger of the two directed a question my way. Before I knew it, the three of us were involved in a deep but innocent conversation. Just prior to deplaning, the older of the two ladies asked for my business card.

Not knowing her motive, I told her that I didn't have any. She then proceeded to tell me that she found me attractive and would like to get to know me better. I must have turned three shades of red. I was so taken aback, I didn't know what to say. My palms began to sweat and my ears felt like they were on fire. I couldn't believe that someone other than my wife would find me attractive. I quickly informed her that I was happily married with six children. She chuckled as she told me that she wasn't interested in marriage, she just wanted to get to know me better.

For the next few days, I couldn't get this experience out of my mind. I don't consider myself attractive and the fact that someone other than my wife found me attractive was a bit intriguing. What did she like about me? Did she really think I was good-looking? Perhaps she didn't notice my large ears. Why would a stranger be so bold and audacious? Several questions ruminated through my mind as I contemplated the matter.

In the Book of Genesis we are taught that God made man in His own image. In the likeness of God were all men and women created. Since we are created after the image of God, we are all offspring of a glorious and magnificent Father in Heaven.

"And God saw every thing that he had made, and, behold, it was very good" (Genesis 1:31).

Our bodies are a divine gift from God, created in a celestial manner. To say we are merely attractive is an understatement at best. We are all spirit children of Heavenly Father, created with wholesome, precious and beautiful attributes.

The older I get, the more I realize just how opposite men and women really are. Though we were both created in the image and likeness of God, we are opposite in so many ways. Heavenly Father knew how important it was to instill opposite qualities within a man and a woman. These opposite qualities create a dynamic force of attraction toward one another. Most men and women are flattered by positive comments from the opposite sex. Though we might experience some embarrassment, positive reinforcement about our appearance or personality has a way of building confidence and self-esteem. As innocent as these comments might seem, they become dangerous words of encouragement and enticement. If you receive a complement regarding your appearance, personality or any other attribute, acknowledge the gesture and then put it aside. Don't get caught up in superficial comments. Of course you're beautiful, God made you that way.

In today's world, more men and women are working side by side than at any other time. We council together, strategize together, dine together and travel together. We spend more time with our co-workers than we do with our own spouses and families. Relationships develop and the opportunity for transgression presents itself. The majority of extramarital affairs in the United States begin within the workplace. We cannot be naïve, and we must take precautions to safeguard ourselves.

SET PARAMETERS

While serving as the Priest Quorum Adviser, I had the opportunity to experience a fifty-mile hike with twelve energetic young men. In preparation for our trip, we held several meetings to plan, organize and establish safety parameters for our youth. Our hike would take us fifty miles up the coast of Washington. We would hike trails, climb hills, cross rock cliffs, and repel down ravines.

Many dangers would surely greet us if we neglected to establish and follow certain safety parameters.

As our journey began, we were instructed to pay close attention to the tide tables. A map was given to us that clearly outlined the locations and times of high tide. We were warned to carefully plan out our trek, as to avoid being caught in the middle of a high-tide situation. The consequences of being in the wrong place at the wrong time could be devastating.

As we entered our third day, my left hip became so sore and weak that I could barely walk. My pace slowed and I began to lag behind the others. Instead of calling out for help, I continued to battle through the adversities caused by my weak hip. Before long, I lost sight of my young men and I found myself caught on a jagged cliff. It didn't take too long to realize that I was in the wrong place at the wrong time. The tide rose with each set of waves. At the rate the tide was rising, I figured that the water would reach me within fifteen minutes. I didn't have the strength to get out of harm's way. If only I had followed our safety parameters and adhered to the tide tables.

Within a few minutes, I saw one of my Priests climbing back over the rocks toward me. Once he reached me, he grabbed my fifty-pound pack and said, "Brother McNaughton, let me help you get out of here." I was overcome with emotions as I unloaded my fifty-pound burden on my young Priest. Though my hip was still ailing, I was able to follow his footsteps over the cliff and away from danger.

When working with the opposite sex, you must set and adhere to safety parameters. You must never allow yourselves to be caught in the wrong place at the wrong time. If you wade in pools of temptation, you will drift away from shore, allowing Satan to engulf you with tides of transgression.

God has instilled within each of us a sacred power to procreate. Like Adam and Eve, married couples have a sacred calling to multiply and replenish the earth. To accommodate this commandment, God blessed each of us with an attraction and desire toward the opposite sex. "Therefore shall a man leave his father and mother, and shall cleave unto his wife, and they shall be one flesh" (Genesis 2:24). To be one flesh, this attraction and desire must remain within the holy bonds of marriage.

Infidelity among husbands and wives is the greatest form of trauma to the modern family. More tears are shed due to infidelity than death. Hearts are broken and lives are shattered. Married couples must discipline themselves, and harness their sexual desires for only their spouse.

Over the past twenty years I have worked in the beauty care industry. This industry is heavily populated with single and married women. Throughout my career, I have implemented several safety parameters to keep myself safe while working with the opposite sex. By incorporating these practices, I have avoided temptation while at the same time fulfilling my job responsibilities.

Matthew S. McNaughton

TRAVELING WITH CO-WORKERS

Several years ago, I boarded a flight from Chicago to San Diego to attend a national sales meeting. Seated next to me was one of my female employees. I thought it would be convenient to sit together so we could review reports and discuss the business in her territory. After an hour of discussing business, my employee dozed off. As time passed, I noticed that her head was falling gradually toward my right shoulder. Each time her head would get too close, I would find a way to wake her up. At one point during the flight, the airplane experienced severe turbulence. Without thinking, my female employee grabbed my right arm and held on for several minutes. The turbulence was nerve racking, but her hand on my arm was extremely uncomfortable. Once the turbulence stopped, the flight attendant approached our row and asked if my wife would like a meal. I informed the flight attendant that she was a co-worker and not my wife. She apologized and then restated her question by asking if my partner would be interested in a meal. That line wasn't much better.

On the surface, the interaction between the two of us may have appeared to be intimate. The fact that we were sitting together and involved in conversation was reason enough for some to assume we were married.

After that experience, I realized that I had to establish some standards while traveling with the opposite sex. Because 60% of my employees were female, I prayerfully considered every facet of my responsibilities. I needed to know for myself what was appropriate behavior and what was not. There couldn't be any gray areas; it had to be black and white.

The following are a few essential rules for the road while traveling with co-workers of the opposite sex.

1. Never sit together while flying on an airplane or any other form of transportation. Make sure all business related issues are handled prior to your travels. If you must discuss business during your travels, secure aisle seats across from one another. The space between the two of you will properly allow conversation without producing an uncomfortable situation.

2. Do not make your hotel reservation at the same time. Allow your coworker to be responsible for his or her own reservation. Many hotels will book a certain block of rooms at the same time. If you make your reservation together, your rooms might be located together. Always see that your room is on a different floor or at least a comfortable distance from your co-worker.

3. Never enter the room of a co-worker for any reason. If you have business to tend to, make a trip to the hotel business center or take care of your business in the lobby.

4. Try to avoid one-on-one dining. If you must dine with a coworker of the opposite sex, make sure you eat in a busy, well-lit restaurant. Make your dinner a business engagement. Bring reports, assignments or any job related issue to discuss. If you do not make this a business engagement, it will result in a personal engagement. Keep all conversation focused on the business at hand.

5. Review your weekly itinerary with your spouse. Never leave home without supplying your spouse with the name and phone number of the hotel in which you are staying.

6. Your spouse should know whom you are working with and where you will be staying.

FLIRTING

Being flirtatious with the opposite sex is one of the first steps toward infidelity. Flirting can be both tangible and intangible. Tangible flirting can be a simple touch of the hand, a pat on the back or even removing lint from clothing.

At a recent national meeting, I witnessed a married man removing a speck of dirt off the cheek of a female coworker. The speck was so small; he was unable to remove it with his thumb and index finger. He then grabbed a tissue and gently removed the speck. After he successfully removed the fragment, the female coworker whispered; "thank-you, you're so sweet."

Some might classify this act as a form of kindness or thoughtfulness. If his wife was present, I don't believe she would view her husband's actions as a gesture of kindness. Nor do I believe that the female coworker would comment how sweet he was. His actions along with hers were both intimate and inappropriate.

When I began my career in 1980, I made a commitment that I would never embrace a female co-worker. I was known throughout the company as the "handshaker."

I set a standard for myself that was recognized, understood and respected by all my peers. During a sales conference in Washington, D.C, I was introduced to a lady from our finance department. As she reached over to give me a hug, one of my female employees stuck her hand out and said: "My boss doesn't hug, he shakes hands." I felt a little embarrassed, but was so thankful for her intervention.

The people we interact with at work come from all walks of life and various backgrounds. Some are raised in environments where physical forms of affection are the norm. Some are more stoical in their behavior. In today's world, it's imperative that we are extremely careful when interacting with those of the opposite sex.

Several years ago, one of my employees filed a complaint of sexual harassment against another. After investigating the allegation, it was discovered that a comment relating to a new hairstyle was made. In speaking with the accused, he informed me that he only gave her a simple complement about how much he liked her new hairstyle. The accuser validated a portion of his testimony but not his intent. She informed me that he put his arm around her and whispered in her ear how beautiful she looked in her new hairstyle. She felt uncomfortable due to his flirtatious manner and considered his remarks inappropriate and a form of sexual harassment.

Most flirting among men and women is wrapped in forms of words and phrases. Engaging in playful and teasing conversation is most prevalent. Flirtatious talk can be enticing and alluring. What begins as innocent and playful dialogue will eventually escalate to intimate and dangerous conversation. The following story will illustrate my point:

Matthew S. McNaughton

On a hot summer day in June of 1965, I was playing in an open field with my best friend. We were seriously involved in the pursuit of lizards and butterflies. As we sat down for a little break, I noticed several books of matches lying in the dirt. Like most seven-year-olds, I was drawn to the matches and desired to light one.

Each time I attempted to light a match, I would break the stem. Because my friend was a couple years older than I was and also his parents smoked, he was a master at the craft. After a few quick lessons, I was up and running. I lit one match after another. Before long, I was lighting two at a time and then three. The fun escalated to the point where I lit a whole book of matches at the same time. At one point, a gust of wind came through and ignited a portion of the dry field.

We tried as hard as we could to put out the fire. We stomped on it with our bare feet, threw dirt on it, and tried to smother it with our shirts. Nothing seemed to work as the fire grew bigger and bigger. I felt that my only option was to run and hide. I ran home and quickly disposed of my smoke filled clothes. Within a few minutes, the whines of sirens could be heard. I knew I would be in big trouble if caught. What seemed as innocent fun, suddenly turned into my darkest hour. Because of my carelessness, I burned several acres of open field, killed wildlife, destroyed tress and even burned a portion of a barn. I cried for days as I suffered the consequences of my action.

I learned firsthand the pains and sufferings that come from playing with matches. Towering infernos begin with a simple spark. Because of this experience, I have developed a deep respect for fire and always take extra precautions when dealing with barbecues, fireplaces, campfires and fireworks.

Flirtatious behaviors are those tiny sparks that can escalate to infidelity. Keep your conversations and relationships at a professional level at all times. Avoid sexual innuendoes and never participate in inappropriate stories or jokes.

You can be personable with the opposite sex without engaging in flirtatious conversations. By taking extra cautions with your conversations, you will be admired and respected by both your superiors and peers, while at the same time avoiding the onset to transgression.

LOCK YOUR HEART

Every hour of every day, homes are broken into and precious belongings are stolen. The fallacy is that most of the homes are not actually broken into. The perpetrator finds windows that are open and doors that are unlocked. We have allowed the intruders into our homes, thereby giving them easy access to our precious belongings.

The cautious homeowner will lock all windows and doors and install security alarm systems. By taking these extra precautions, they deter the intruder's advances, thereby safeguarding their family and belongings.

Once marriage is solemnized, only one key to the heart is issued. That key is given to your spouse. Your spouse is the only person authorized to use that key. He or she becomes the sole owner and operator of that sacred key of love and intimacy. Your spouse will never loan or give the key to another person. In order for another person to access your heart, you must successfully steal the key away from your spouse and then personally unlock your heart. Once this is done, you become extremely vulnerable to the advances of the opposite sex. If allowed, the intruder will walk right in and rob you of your most precious and sacred blessings.

Prior to purchasing our home in Chicago, my wife and I toured over a hundred homes. Though many homes were appealing, we wanted to find just the right home that would best suit our family. Once we narrowed our selection down to three, we returned several times to walk the halls, measure the walls and get an overall feeling of the neighborhood. Each home had different qualities and unique characteristics that made it special. However, we had to choose one. After much contemplation, we decided on a home out in the country. Though it didn't have all the amenities and beauty of the other two, it was perfect for our family and met the needs of our personal circumstances.

Upon signing the final papers and receiving the keys, we never looked back at the other homes. Regardless of their beauty, they were no longer important to us. This home was now ours, and we were the sole owners. We were proud of our home and looked forward to many wonderful experiences within its walls. Though the home wasn't perfect, it was indeed perfect for us.

Throughout your life, you will encounter many wonderful, beautiful and endearing people of the opposite sex. You might even see qualities in these individuals that are appealing to you. My wife often tells me that I'm the only person she could ever be married to. Though I love to hear those sentiments, I know that's not an accurate statement. There are thousands of people upon the earth that we could fall in love with and find compatible. But after you find that one special person and enter the holy covenant of marriage, you must lock your heart and never look backward or forward in regard to relationships. I often tell my wife that she is perfect; meaning she is perfect for me.

Lock your heart and give the key to your spouse. By doing so you will safeguard your precious possessions and experience joy, love and eternal happiness with your companion.

CAUTIOUS COUNSEL

We have all heard the cliché, "life wasn't meant to be easy, just worth it." Every human being experiences difficulty from time to time. President Hinckley describes life as an old-time rail journey—delays, sidetracks, smoke, dust cinders and jolts, interspersed only occasionally by beautiful vistas and thrilling bursts of speed.

Frequently, people come to work burdened down with personal trials. Most people are private about their personal lives and prefer to keep their problems to themselves. Others are more open and will confide in friends and seek counsel from those they respect and trust.

A lady who was experiencing difficulties with her marriage approached a colleague of mine for advice. Over a period of several weeks, he listened to her problems and gave her wise counsel. He also took the opportunity to share with her several principles of the Gospel. After a few discussions with the lady, an invitation was extended to have the missionaries come by to teach her and her husband about the Church. She declined to have the missionary discussions but continued to seek his counsel and advice. Over a period of several weeks, the lady found solace and reassurance from her male coworker.

What began as innocent counseling, was beginning to develop into something much different. As time passed, feelings of admiration and compassion began to build between the two individuals. These feelings of compassion developed into infatuation. Infatuation turned to infidelity.

A righteous desire to counsel an injured woman ended in pain and heartache for two families. No one is immune from Satan's temptations. Even in the midst of a righteous endeavor, people can fall into transgression.

The best advice to give someone of the opposite sex is to seek professional counsel. Never meddle in co-workers' private affairs. Keep all conversations centered on your work and maintain a professional relationship at all times.

By adhering to these standards, you will maintain a wholesome and professional relationship with all individuals of the opposite sex. Lock your heart, give your spouse sole possession of the key, and remember, "opposites mustn't attract."

Chapter Five
SHAPE UP

The reason why some people fail in their attempt to lose weight and get in shape is not due to a lack of ability but rather a lack of knowledge, determination, discipline and focus. Throughout my life, I have gained and lost a thousand pounds. For every diet plan I've failed to conquer, there were a hundred reasons. My number-one reason was the fact that I traveled. Let's face it, it's difficult to stick to a diet while away from home. How many times have you caught yourself saying, "I don't care what I eat, I'm on vacation." We have a tendency to view food as a reward. We treat ourselves with unhealthy and fatty foods for a job well done. This philosophy is amplified while traveling on business.

As a young college athlete, I had no problem keeping myself in good physical condition. I was on a strenuous weight-lifting program and ran two miles each day. My diet was pretty simplistic, and never did I stray. I was on a "sea food diet" meaning, see food and eat it. I ate everything I could get my hands on, and not once did I worry about excessive carbohydrates or fat grams. My metabolism was in overdrive. I was strong, energetic, healthy, lean and young. Little did I realize how much my physical condition would change over the next few years.

Shortly after marriage I began my career as a traveling sales representative. My diet remained the same as it did during my college years, however, my physical activity came to a halt. I had become a classic couch potato, using different excuses and reasons why I couldn't exercise: a shoulder injury, my travel schedule, church callings, I'll start next Monday. Until finally I woke up one morning, looked in the mirror and realized I was fat.

Being overweight and out of shape was not my idea. I never planned on being fat. It was certainly not something that happened overnight. In just two years, I allowed my physical body to balloon up to 245 pounds. My waist went from thirty-four inches to forty inches. My face was full, and I developed a second chin. I found it difficult to bend over to tie my shoes. I was fat and I knew it.

What I allowed to happen to my body was not something I would ever allow to happen to my job or my responsibilities at home or church. I became physically lazy and was neglecting my body. This wasn't the way I approached any other aspect of my life. Why then was I so undisciplined when it came to my physical body?

One evening while I was sitting in my hotel room talking to my wife on the phone, I glanced over to the mirror and saw a very large mass of blubber sitting on my lap. I couldn't believe what I was looking at. My stomach certainly couldn't be that big. I thought that perhaps the mirror was warped and was distorting my actual proportions. Unfortunately, this wasn't the case. Right at that time, I made a commitment to my wife that I was going to change my life.

I made a decision that I was going to lose weight, get in shape and run a marathon. Up until that time in my life, the longest distance I had ever run was three miles. Was I insane to believe that I could run 26.2 miles? I was angry with myself because of my poor physical condition, and I became totally committed and focused. Nothing was going to get in my way of accomplishing this goal.

EATING HABITS

The first thing I had to change was my eating habits. Because of my travels, I developed a lifestyle of driving through fast-food restaurants. It was fast, convenient, affordable and tasted pretty good. Wherever my travels took me, I could always count on finding a fast-food restaurant to satisfy my appetite.

The fast-food industry is a $129 billion business. More than half the money spent on fast food rolls in through the drive-thru lane. The drive-thru concept was implemented to increase revenues and to meet the needs of the consumer. The fast-food industry wanted more money and the American consumer wanted more convenience.

The fast-food giants are trying to make life as easy and convenient for the American consumer. Most fast-food restaurants now accept debit and charge cards. Over 400 McDonald's in the Chicago area have implemented a concept called "Speedpass." The consumer simply waves a tiny speedpass wand, which fits on a key ring over a sensor. The payment is recorded and automatically debits a credit card. Whatever it takes to stimulate profits, the fast-food giants are eager to explore. Easy and convenient? Perhaps. Healthy and wise? Perhaps not.

A popular country song refers to fast food as a "ninety-nine cent heart attack." The song is catchy and cute, but the lyrics are deadly true. The majority of fast food is loaded with excessive calories, fats and sodium. An excess of these ingredients will increase your body fat, raise your cholesterol and boost blood pressure. The last thing the traveling professional needs more of is hypertension!

According to a University of Delaware Food and Nutrition Fact, "Sodium plays a major role in the maintenance of blood volume and blood pressure. It is also needed for nerve transmission and muscle contraction. However, as valuable as sodium is, the body requires very little. The link between sodium and hypertension is well established. About half of the patients with hypertension and thirty percent of the general public are known as 'salt sensitive.' Health officials agree that a low-to-moderate sodium diet helps in the prevention of hypertension. The National Academy of Sciences indicates that an adequate level of sodium for the average adult is between 1100–3300 mg per day. Many people consume two to three times this amount."

However, not all fast food is bad. The variety of foods available through fast-food outlets has expanded in recent years. In some restaurants you can now order fiber-rich soups, salads and vegetables, such as potatoes, carrot sticks, and corn-on-the-cob. In my research of all the fast-food chains, I found that there are several good and nutritious foods. If you need a quick meal while on the road, there are some fast foods worth crossing the street for. The following is a list of the fast foods I recommend that are reasonably low in calories and fat grams. Though the fat grams and calories are moderately low, many meals listed are still a little high in sodium.

Restaurant	Meal	Calories	Total Fat (g)	Sodium (mg)
Arby's	Light Roasted Turkey Deluxe	260	7	1,260
	Grilled Chicken BBQ	390	13	1,000
	Light Roast Beef Deluxe	300	10	830
	Light Roasted Chicken Deluxe	280	6	780
	Roast Chicken Salad (Low-Cal Dressing)	170	3	1,130
Burger King	Broiled Chicken Salad (Light Dressing)	230	11	830
Dairy Queen	Grilled Chicken Sandwich	310	10	1,040
Hardee's	Grilled Chicken Sandwich	350	11	950
	Grilled Chicken Salad	220	3	1,190
Jack in the Box	Chicken Fajita Pita	280	9	840
	Garden Chicken Salad (Low-Cal Dressing)	230	11	1,090
KFC	BBQ Chicken Sandwich	260	8	780
McDonald's	Grilled Chicken Salad (Fat-Free Dressing)	170	2	570
	Chicken Fajita	190	7	360
Subway	Chicken or turkey Sub (6")	320	5	1,190
	Roast Beef Sub (6")	300	5	940
	Club or Ham Sub (6")	310	5	1,340
	Tuna Sub w/light mayo (6")	390	15	940

Restaurant	Meal	Calories	Total Fat (g)	Sodium (mg)
	Roast Beef or Chicken Salad	180	4	1,230
Taco Bell	Bean Burrito	380	12	1,140
Wendy's	Grilled Chicken Sandwich	310	8	790
	Grilled Chicken Salad	270	8	1,020
	Baked Potato (sour cream and chives)	380	6	40
	Chili Small (no cheese)	190	6	670

Obesity is the number-two most serious public health issue in America, second only to smoking. Over 51 million people in America are obese. Obesity is defined as being thirty or more pounds over a healthy weight, which varies by height. Weighing too much contributes to diabetes, arthritis, heart disease, depression and other related ailments. Each year, an estimated 300,000 Americans die of obesity-related conditions. Americans spend more than $30 billion a year on weight-loss products and programs. And yet our nation has never been fatter and less healthy.

The single greatest cause of obesity is lack of knowledge, control and focus. We eat for more reasons than just to sustain life. We eat when we're bored, we eat when we're depressed, we eat to be social, and we eat for pleasure. Eating can become habitual. How many times do you find yourself opening the pantry or refrigerator out of habit? The majority of overweight people simply eat too much of the wrong foods and exercise too little.

Food is essential to sustain life. Food provides us with energy. This energy is carried within the molecules of three basic nutrients: carbohydrates, fats and proteins. When our body breaks them down, energy is released. This energy is used for all our basic body functions. Without food we become weak, starve our bodies of nutrients and eventually die.

Curbing our appetite for fatty and unhealthy foods takes discipline and self-control. When we change our diet and reduce our food intake, we can experience temporary withdrawals, headaches, mood swings and, of course, hunger pangs.

We read in the Book of Mormon about the many trials and tribulations that Lehi and his family experienced. Through it all, Father Lehi remained faithful in the midst of adversity. However, on one occasion it was recorded that Lehi did murmur against the Lord.

> And it came to pass that as I, Nephi went forth to slay food, behold, I did break my bow, which was made of fine steel; and after I did break my bow, behold, my brethren were angry with me because of the loss of my bow, for we did obtain no food.
>
> And it came to pass that we did return without food to our families, and being much fatigued, because of their journeying, they did suffer much for the want of food.
>
> And it came to pass that Laman and Lemuel and the sons of Ishmael did begin to murmur exceedingly, because of their sufferings and afflictions in the wilderness; and also my father began to murmur against the Lord his God; yea, and they were all exceedingly sorrowful, even that they did murmur against the Lord. (1 Nephi 16:18-20)

Lehi and his family didn't eat for a time because they couldn't. They murmured because of their sufferings and afflictions due to fatigue and hunger. I'm sure Lehi and his family experienced withdrawals, headaches, mood swings and hunger pangs.

Of all the adversities that Lehi experienced while in the wilderness, it was the lack of food that caused him to murmur against the Lord. Food is a necessity, and without it, we will suffer and die.

Around dinnertime, I usually say to my wife "Honey, what's for dinner, I'm starved." To this day, I have never experienced true hunger. I have gone a couple of days without food, but no longer. I have experienced little hunger pangs now and then, but never have I experienced true hunger. I will never know what Lehi and his family experienced, but I do know how important food was for their well-being.

Food is one of the greatest blessings the Lord has bestowed upon us. Because it is so abundant in most parts of the world, we often take food for granted. We eat what we want, when we want. We eat foods that taste good, but not necessarily foods that are good for our bodies. The Lord has given us specific guidelines in regard to our diet.

> And again, verily I say unto you, all wholesome herbs God hath ordained for the constitution, nature, and use of man.
>
> Every herb in the season thereof, and every fruit in the season thereof; all these to be used with prudence and thanksgiving.

Yea, flesh also of beast and of the fouls of the air, I, the Lord, hath ordained for the use of man with thanksgiving; nevertheless they are to be used sparingly.

And it is pleasing unto me that they should not be used, only in times of winter, or of cold, or famine.

All grain is good for the food of man; as also the fruit of the vine; that which yieldeth fruit, whether in the ground or above the ground.

And all saints who remember to keep and do these sayings, walking in obedience to the commandments, shall receive health in their naval and marrow to their bones.

And shall find wisdom and great treasures of knowledge, even hidden treasures.

And shall run and not be weary, and shall walk and not faint.

And I the Lord give unto them a promise, that the destroying angel shall pass by them, as the children of Israel, and not slay them. Amen.
(D&C 89:10–13 and 16–21)

    As I embarked on my new goals to lose weight, get in shape and run a marathon, I considered the manner in which I was going to accomplish this. I decided that I was not going to resort to any special diet program or pills. For me, taking diet pills to lose weight and body fat was the same as taking steroids to gain weight and muscle. I felt in my heart that it was wrong and against the Word of Wisdom.

I contemplated my eating habits and made note of the foods I ate that were not listed in the Word of Wisdom. I then analyzed their nutritional value, fat grams and calories.

The following are a few of the foods I ate on a daily basis:
- Ice Cream
- Soda Pop
- Milk Shakes
- Potato Chips
- Candy Bars
- Array of Desserts
- Fast Foods of Every Kind

Once I analyzed their nutritional value, calories and fat grams, I was surprised that I only weighed 245 pounds. Not only did I eat the wrong foods but also I ate too much food. After additional research, I also learned that I ate some foods for the wrong reasons.

Any activity that requires monitoring, such as following a strict diet, is harder to do during times of stress. In other words, when things go bad, dietary lawlessness can set it, and you can find yourself craving the "forbidden foods." In my case it was chocolate and other sweets. We clearly don't always eat based on hunger. People may indulge to fulfill a psychological need.

I'm not alone in my craving for sweets. The typical American consumes an astonishing thirty-four teaspoons of sugar per day from food and beverages, especially soft drinks. Daily calorie consumption has jumped from 1,830 ten years ago to 2,200 today. Our lifestyles have become complex and our eating habits are out of control.

TAKING CONTROL

One day a neighbor stopped by to chat as he was walking his dog. I noticed that the dog was extremely overweight. During our conversation, I made a comment about the size of his pooch. He said:, "I know he's a little chubby, but he has a huge appetite." I informed him that he needs to keep his dog's paws out of the fridge. He looked at me and said, "Oh I get it. You think that I feed him too much."

As adults, we have full autonomy as to what we put in our mouth. We are not forced to overeat or eat the wrong foods. If you are overweight, you and only you must make a decision to do something about it. You need to take action. You need to take control of your appetite and change your eating habits.

The following are the steps I took to lose the weight and regain my health and stamina.

1. I eliminated from my diet the foods and beverages that I knew were not good for me. These were the foods and beverages that I craved for one reason or another. I called them my "forbidden foods." Have you ever noticed that you hardly ever crave good wholesome foods? It's always the fatty foods or foods that have no nutritional value that our body seems to crave. For me it was ice cream, soda pop, milk shakes, candy bars, potato chips, desserts and, of course, fast food. Analyze your diet and eliminate these so-called forbidden foods.

2. I developed a habit of drinking water in place of soft drinks. I began my day by drinking twelve ounces of water. Not only is drinking enough water throughout the day good for you but it can also decrease your short-term hunger pangs. Keeping your body hydrated will allow you to think more clearly and will improve your daily performance.

3. I began a thirty-minute cardiovascular workout each morning, either on my stationary bike or an outdoor run. By exercising in the morning on an empty stomach, your body burns more fat than if you first ate breakfast. Exercising in the morning also kick-starts your metabolism for the rest of the day. I'll shed more light on this topic, in relation to traveling, at the end of this chapter.

4. I ate a breakfast full of lean protein, complex carbohydrates and fiber. This could include a bowl of oatmeal with raisins, an egg omelet and a small glass of orange juice. Studies have proven that people who eat a healthy, balanced breakfast every day have significantly lower body fat. A good supply of protein for breakfast will keep your blood sugar steady throughout the morning, so you won't have any excess hunger pangs.

5. I started taking a multivitamin that contains antioxidants such as vitamin C, vitamin E and selenium to make up for any dietary lapses.

6. I kept a bag of trail mix with unsalted peanuts, raisins and Rice Chex® along with an apple at my office or in my car. Snacking lightly throughout the day helps keep your blood sugar and energy levels up. Smart snacks will also help prevent your metabolism from slowing down, which will aid continued fat loss. Unsalted peanuts are full of protein and healthy fats, which will keep you going without causing fatigue. Snacking on peanuts will also satisfy your hunger pangs. A survey of the U. S. Department of Agriculture data showed that regular peanut eaters had better muscle-to-fat ratios than others.

7. If I was working in my office or traveling within town, I packed my own lunch. As long as I didn't eat any of the "forbidden foods" or an excess of food, I didn't worry about the content of my lunch. I did cut mayonnaise out of my diet, and I added a stalk of celery that was lightly coated with peanut butter.

8. While traveling out of town, I had several choices for lunch. An excellent lunch entrée would be a bean burrito with chicken or chili with beans and beef. Beans are an underrated weight-loss food; they block fat absorption, lower blood cholesterol, make you feel full and are loaded with antioxidants, B vitamins and minerals. You can find these two meals at Taco Bell and Wendy's. You can also go to a deli for a healthy "non-fried" lunch. If you can't find a deli, stop by a supermarket. Most supermarkets have a deli section where you can order a nutritious meal. Just make sure you stay away from your "forbidden foods."

9. Dinner can be the make-or-break meal while on the road. Your mind has left work and is now centered on your appetite. You put in a good day and dinner can serve as your physical reward. If you're eating with friends or colleagues at a restaurant, be careful! It's easy to forget about your diet when eating among friends. Incorporate the following do's and don'ts while eating your evening meal in a restaurant:

DON'TS
a. Don't eat any hors d'oeuvres.
b. Don't eat any breads or rolls. If you just can't resist, only eat one plain slice.
c. Don't eat pastas and heavy cream sauces. You don't need a lot of extra carbs for energy this late in the day.
d. Don't eat any desserts.
e. Don't eat after 7:00 PM.
f. Don't eat your entire meal just because it's there. The typical dinner plate in most restaurants has grown in size from 10 1/2 inches to 12 1/2 inches. I decide before I begin eating how much I'm going to consume. I actually draw a line through my portion and once I'm through, I quickly call the waiter over to pick up my plate. I have learned to eat until I'm comfortable and not until I'm stuffed.

DO'S
a. Drink plenty of water prior to dinner.
b. A cup of soup is a good way to begin your meal, as long as it is not cream-based.
c. Six to eight ounces of grilled fish is a terrific food full of high-quality protein as well as fatty acids. Fish is healthy for your heart and blocks joint inflammation.
d. Beef and chicken are also good sources of protein. However, we are informed in the scriptures to eat it sparingly.
e. Have plenty of colorful vegetables on the side. Order a salad with lowfat dressing, broccoli and half a sweet potato. You can consume all the salad and fiber-rich vegetables you desire.

f. Use good judgment and don't allow the environment of the restaurant to tempt you to overeat or eat the wrong foods.

EXERCISE

I explained earlier in this chapter about the importance of physical exercise during the morning hours. I will now share with you the benefits of physical exercise during the evening hours.

When traveling, make sure you stay in a hotel that offers a weight room. If your hotel does not have a weight room, you can get a day pass at the local gym. If you feel uncomfortable going to a public gym, or it's not convenient, put your running shoes on and jog for your evening workout. Depending on my schedule, I would catch another thirty-minute workout prior to dinner or later in the evening around 9:00 PM. Weightlifting or any aerobic exercise consumes calories, raises your metabolism and builds muscle. Exercise will also release endorphins that can combat depression and relieve stress.

Working out in the evening is also a great diversion from temptation. Breaking up your evening with a workout will stimulate your mind and body. Your mind will focus on your health instead of inappropriate desires. I have also found that I sleep better when I add an exercise routine in the evening.

You can't work out if you don't pack appropriate clothing. After packing my scriptures, my running shoes and workout clothing are next.

Physical conditioning requires a great deal of self-discipline and focus. Establishing goals and charting your progress are paramount. Once I made the decision to change my life, I established three goals: lose thirty-five pounds, get in shape and run a marathon. I wrote these goals down and plastered them all over my office walls.

I purchased a good reliable scale and weighed myself every Monday morning. I chose Monday, because the weekends were always the most difficult days to stick to my diet. I was motivated to eat healthy during the weekends because I knew I had an appointment with my scale every Monday morning. After weighing myself, I wrote my weight down on a calendar. I kept this calendar in a prominent location to remind me of my goal.

I also charted my workouts. Whether it was lifting weights or running, I kept a daily log of my exercise activity. I'm motivated by positive results. As my performance increased, my desire to do better increased as well.

Within three months, my weight dropped from 240 pounds to 220 pounds. I went from jogging 100 yards to jogging five miles. I noticed my life changing before my eyes. After ten months, I was at my desired weight of 205 pounds.

And now for my ultimate goal; run a marathon. This goal was a bit more challenging. Each year beginning with 1988, I trained for the St. George Marathon. With each attempt, I suffered from a condition called posterior tibial tendonitis (inner-ankle tendon inflammation) that kept me from obtaining my goal. With each setback I became more and more discouraged, but I was focused on my goal and refused to yield to failure. Finally in 1998 at the age of 40, I accomplished my goal. At 6'2" and 205, I completed my first St. George Marathon and crossed the finish line at 4:55:18. Tears of emotion rolled down my cheeks. I did something that many people said I couldn't.

To this day I don't consider myself a runner, however I did return to St. George the following year to better my time.

Take care of your physical body. Don't abuse it or misuse it. It's a glorious gift from God our Father. Be wise and use wisdom in your eating habits and exercise routines.

Keeping your body in good physical condition will increase your mental capacity, spiritual awareness and emotional stability. Your outward appearance will reflect your inward health. Your overall attitude will change for the better and your life will be prolonged. You will be more productive at work, church and home.

If I can do it, I know that you can do it. I learned that success will come if you're patient, determined and focused. Shape Up!

Chapter Six
FIRST THINGS FIRST
"HONORING AND FULFILLING CHURCH AND FAMILY COMMITMENTS"

After seven years of constant travel, I was ready to move on to something else. I was twenty-nine years old, and my little family had grown to four children. Missing special events and family activities became the norm. I had turned into a "part-time" daddy, and I could feel the strain that my travels were placing on my family. My life was out of balance due to my travels, and I was losing touch with my family and church responsibilities. I felt that the only choice I had to balance my life was to change my career.

After six months of prayer and consideration, my wife and I decided that I should pursue another profession. Within a short period of time, I received a job offer that was commensurate with my skills, while at the same time eliminating my travels. I was excited for the opportunity and looked forward to getting reacquainted with my family. Unfortunately, my new job would require my family to relocate to a new area.

At the time, I was serving on the high council and thoroughly enjoyed my responsibilities. Though my travel schedule was quite demanding, I did the best I could to tend to the needs of my family and fulfill my church responsibilities. I placed a tremendous amount of pressure and guilt on myself because I wasn't able to give 100% to my family or the Church. I felt in my heart that changing professions would allow me to devote the necessary time to my family and the Lord, while at the same time relieving undo pressure and guilt.

Two days prior to giving my notice to my current employer, our little world turned upside down.

General Authorities from Salt Lake were in town to call a new stake presidency. Because I was on the high council, and in keeping with proper protocol, I was given a worthiness interview. Going into the interview I was calm and relaxed. There was nothing for me to worry about. I was very young, inexperienced in the gospel, and I was going to move in a few weeks. I breezed through my three-minute interview, picked up my kids from grandma's house and broke my fast at a local restaurant.

Shortly after returning home, my telephone rang. On the other end of the line was my stake president. My heart sank to my stomach as I heard him say, "Brother McNaughton, can you and your lovely wife be at the stake center by 3:30?" My wife could tell by the tone of my voice that something serious just took place. She asked me what was wrong. I gently told her that she needed to put on a dress and accompany me to the stake center. She was adamant in her resolve to know what had just taken place. I told her I didn't know, but I did know that our future was not going to unfold like we thought.

Upon arriving at the stake center, we were escorted into the stake president's office. As we entered the office, I saw the two General Authorities, Bishop and Sister Christensen and President and Sister Ensign. I knew at that time that I was being called as the second counselor in the stake presidency. I was overcome with feelings of inadequacy. I was humbled, frightened and confused. Why was this happening when we spent the last six months praying about a new profession? I wanted to pursue my new career, eliminate my travel and relocate to a different city. I had it all planned out. However, when Elder Cuthbert asked if I would be willing to accept the call, I responded quickly and affirmatively; yes!

As we departed the stake center and returned home, my wife said, "So, I guess I should probably unpack?"

Six months of searching, pondering and praying came down to a three-minute interview. Prior to being called into the stake presidency, I wanted to do what I felt was right, and not necessarily what was right. I believed that the only way to change my personal circumstances was to change my job. I wasn't in tune with the Spirit and I allowed my personal feelings to interfere with the "simple truth."

I was becoming resentful toward my job and even the church for stealing precious time away from my family. After serving in the stake presidency for three months, I discovered what the "simple truth" was. The problem wasn't due to my time away from home; it was due to my time while at home.

Following an extremely busy and hectic month, I sat down and analyzed how I spent my time. In my mind, I figured I spent the entire month either at the stake center or away on business. After evaluating the month, I learned that I spent more time at home than I did away. I was surprised and embarrassed to learn how poorly I managed my time while at home.

The more responsibilities one has, the more organized one must become. The most effective and successful people in the world are the ones with little to no time. However, when extra responsibilities or duties come their way, they seem to find the time to accomplish the task.

The first thing I had to do was to change my focus. Instead of focusing on my time away from home, I started to focus on my time while at home.

As members of the Church, we have all heard this saying a million times, "Family First." What does that really mean? Are we to actually place our family above any church meeting or activity? The family is the most important unit in the Church and tending to the needs of the family is paramount. However, the family is usually the first thing to take a back seat when duty calls. The following story will, unfortunately, illustrate my point:

> Back in 1988, my six-year-old son Shawn was a huge Steve Young fan. The San Francisco Forty-Niners were coming to town during the off season to play a charity basketball game against the Oakland Raiders. My son's first-grade teacher was dating one of the defensive backs for the Forty-Niners, and she scheduled a time and place for Shawn to meet his idol. My son was so excited and could hardly wait. There was only one problem; my wife was ill and I had a church commitment that was in direct conflict with the scheduled meeting. I promised

my son that I would only stay for thirty minutes of the meeting and then return home in time to take him to meet Steve Young.

Once I arrived at the stake center, I became totally involved in my assignment. I watched the clock tick away, and I knew it would be difficult to leave the meeting. My thoughts were centered on my "church calling" and not my "family calling." Before I knew it, an hour and a half had elapsed. I returned home to a devastated little boy. I broke a promise and neglected my most important calling. To this day, I don't recall the purpose of the church meeting or who was in attendance, but I will never forget the pain I brought to a little boy by neglecting my most important calling.

I had to reevaluate my priorities and come to an understanding of what is meant by "family first."

Our most important callings and responsibilities are found within the family. The family unit is by far the most essential organization in the Church. You will never be released or excused from this sacred and eternal calling.

At the end of each week, as I would return from my travels, my children would come running from every corner of the house shouting, "Daddy's home." Oh, how I loved to hear those words. Those words were my cue that I was now entering a place of far greater importance. At your place of work, you are needed. But sad as it may seem, there has never been a man or a woman who, when they leave their daily job for another or when they retire, is not adequately replaced. Things will go on quite well without you. As one man said, "I felt that if I left my company, it would take a month or so and then I'd be replaced, and perhaps they wouldn't even miss me. However, I was wrong. It only took one week."

Our greatest calling is where we are needed most. As parents, you are needed most within the walls of your own home. When you leave your home, you're missed. And until you return, there will be an empty, unfilled space in the hearts of your family. A man and woman's greatest contribution is made within the home, serving their family.

As we consider the phrase, "First Things First," let us therefore be good parents first and everything else second. We must put forth a good effort in our profession and church callings and even a better effort into our families. Our profession never has nor ever will be as important as our families.

Some men and women who spend a great deal of time at work or in church callings take pride in these long hours away from home. Unfortunately, in some cases it is just a way of not going home. You can't expect your spouse to pick up where you left off. You need to go home and tend to the needs of your family.

I've often felt that if I devote many hours to my church calling and profession, the Lord will compensate by taking care of the needs of my family. This logic sounds good but unfortunately is not totally accurate. Faithful church members, even those in prominent positions, do have problems at home. A major cause of these problems may be a lack of parents not attending to "First Things First."

To place the family first doesn't mean to neglect all other responsibilities and only tend to the needs of the family. We are all consumed from day to day with a myriad of responsibilities. To meet the temporal and spiritual needs of the family, we must magnify our church callings and work-related responsibilities. Because of the Church, we become better fathers and mothers, sons and daughters, through service and receiving direction and counsel from our leaders. President Hinckley said:

> "The Lord has given you this glorious Church, His Church, to guide you and direct you, to give you opportunity for growth and experience, to teach you and lead you and encourage you, to make of you His chosen daughter or son, one upon whom He may look with love and with a desire to help.
>
> Let the church be your dear friend. Let it be your great companion. Serve wherever you are called to serve. Do what you are asked to do. Every position you hold will add to your capacity. Every bit of service will bring its own reward."

If you take care of the Lord's work, He will take care of you. If you magnify your church calling, you will be blessed in your personal life as well as your professional life. The key is to learn and understand the principle of "First Things First."

Placing the family first requires organization and follow-through. We are taught in the Doctrine and Covenants: "Organize yourself; prepare every needful thing." If you organize your responsibilities and follow through with your commitments, you will experience an overwhelming feeling of fulfillment and satisfaction.

To relieve the burdens caused by my extensive travels, I implemented a family monthly calendar. This calendar was the instrument I needed to help me stay focused on my family and remember the importance of "First things First."

MONTHLY CALENDAR

The last Sunday of each month, we sat down as a family and planned out our monthly calendar. We included the entire family and made this an enjoyable event. The first thing we wrote on the calendar was my travel commitments. Every member of the family knew when dad had to be out of town. The next thing to go on the calendar was all church activities and responsibilities. The third item was any school activities or other personal events. Date nights for mom and dad were penciled in, followed by "special date with dad" (Each month I would take one child on a special date for the evening.) Once the calendar was complete, everyone knew where dad was and when he was coming home. The calendar helped each member of the family focus on the "home events" and not the "away events."

The calendar would fluctuate from time to time, however, there were certain non-negotiable items. Any activity involving family-related matters would always take precedence over any unscheduled church, personal or work-related assignment. Certainly there are those unexpected emergencies when I had to respond, but for the most part we stuck to our calendar.

By focusing on your "home time" instead of your "away time," you will find those precious hours that you thought were lost. Your family time will increase in quality and quantity.

ACCEPTING AND FULFILLING CHURCH ASSIGNMENTS

At one time or another, we have all received that call from a member of the bishopric or stake presidency asking for us to meet them in their office. We know that something is up and we begin to contemplate the new calling. You might catch yourself saying, "I hope it's not this, and I hope it's not that." As you drive to the interview, you think about your travel schedule and how that might conflict with your new calling. It's amazing how your travel commitments seem to increase at the time of a new calling.

As the interview proceeds, you hold your "travel commitments" in your back pocket in case you need to use it. If you're happy with the new calling, you readily accept. If the new calling is one that doesn't agree with you, or one that you think might interfere with your travels, you wiggle in your chair and say, "You know, Bishop, I travel every week with my job, and I just don't know if that calling will be compatible with my travel schedule."

In referring to church callings, I often hear the saying: "The Lord doesn't ask for your abilities, only your availability." Because the traveler is not available at times, he or she might acquiesce to the theory that they are exempt from certain callings. This should not be the case.

When a calling comes your way, it's important that you are up front and honest with the person extending the call. Share with them your travel schedule and other commitments. Make sure they understand that you travel out of town and from time to time will be unable to function in your calling.

One of the main reasons why people turn down church callings is because of their fear of not being able to properly fulfill their calling. Active members of the Church want to serve in the Kingdom and give 100% to their calling. If they feel that their personal or professional commitments will keep them from achieving this objective, they prefer to decline the opportunity.

As a traveling businessperson, you need to understand that you will not be able to give 100% to your church calling all the time. If you do the best you can with the time you have, the Lord will bless you in your endeavors.

Don't turn down callings just because you travel. Accept these opportunities and find happiness in serving the Lord. Don't feel guilty for the things you can't do; feel privileged and blessed for the things you can. If you serve righteously and pray for guidance and support, the Lord will help you find a way to accomplish your assignments.

> "I will go and do the things which the Lord hath commanded, for I know that the Lord giveth no commandments unto the children of men, save he shall prepare a way for them that they may accomplish the thing which he commandeth them." (1 Nephi 3:7)

When away on business, use a portion of the evening hours to plan your lesson, prepare your talk or tend to your church responsibilities. Even though you're away from home, you can still magnify your church callings. Pick up the telephone or your cell phone to return calls, set up meetings or confirm appointments. Keep your calls short and to the point. It might cost a little extra, but the blessing for doing so will compensate for any telephone charges you make on the Lord's behalf. President Hinckley said:

> "God bless you with a spirit of serving. If it involves a sacrifice, don't worry about it, because it isn't really sacrifice. That is the marvelous thing. It isn't sacrifice because, when you give, you always gain more than you give."

Sacrifice is the very essence of religion; it is the keystone of happy home life, the basis of true friendship and the foundation of peaceful community living and sound relations among people and nations.

> "Therefore, O ye that embark in the service of God, see that ye serve him with all your heart, might, mind and strength, that ye may stand blameless before God at the last day." (D&C 4:2)

As you implement the principle of "FirstThings First," you will balance out your priorities, therefore allowing you to magnify your callings at home, at work and at church. Feelings of guilt will give way to feelings of gratitude and satisfaction.

Heavenly Father cares very little about the way you make an honorable living. His only concern is how you live. Magnify your church calling and begin with the most important of all organizations, your family.

Chapter Seven
TRAVEL WITH YOUR TESTIMONY

Once we gain a testimony of the Restored Gospel of Jesus Christ, it becomes our responsibility to share that testimony with others.

"Behold, I sent you out to testify and warn the people, and it becometh every man who hath been warned to warn his neighbor." (D&C 88:81)

One of the more difficult commandments for most members of the Church to uphold is to actively share their testimony and invite friends and associates to learn more about the Church. It's difficult because it's uncomfortable, not because it's hard. It's not hard to invite friends to a party, baby shower or over for dinner. But to invite a friend or associate to learn about the Church can be uncomfortable and even awkward at times.

By nature, human beings value relationships. Our lives are centered on the relationships we develop with other human beings. Some relationships take longer to establish than others. Once we feel comfortable within a relationship, we begin to cultivate that relationship through personal interactions, recreation, sacrifice and service. These personal interactions build strong bonds of trust. Because we place such a high value on relationships, we become extremely careful not to say or do anything that might impede that relationship.

Some members of the Church feel that sharing the gospel with friends and associates can hamper a relationship. Many members are more than willing to go the extra mile in regard to church duties and assignments, but when it comes to missionary work, some prefer to take a back seat.

On one occasion, I was told that members of the Church who don't share their testimony, have no testimony. This is not a true statement! The reason why most members of the Church don't invite their friends and associates to learn more about the gospel is because they don't want to place their friendship in jeopardy. Most members assume that their friends and associates will not be interested in learning about the Church. To avoid an uncomfortable situation, many members of the Church remain silent.

Within the heart of every active member of the Church is a burning desire to share the gospel with their friends; they just don't want to offend them in any way. Because of this, members of the Church are very cautious when it comes to doing missionary work.

Prior to my mission I was somewhat influential in the conversion of two individuals who joined the Church. I say somewhat, because I did not directly invite them to learn more about the gospel. I invited them to church functions and activities, but that was the extent of it. I had many opportunities, but I didn't want to risk losing a friend. Once these two individuals were baptized, they both chastised me for not sharing my testimony with them and my desire for them to learn more about the Church.

Once I entered the mission field, it became very easy for me to share the gospel. Yes, it was my full-time responsibility and I was set apart for this assignment, but I was also among people who I didn't know. I didn't worry about losing a friend or offending a neighbor. Most of the time, I was quite bold in my efforts to share the truth and bring souls unto Christ. The interesting fact was this: I didn't make one enemy for the entire two years I served the Lord. Instead, I developed friendships and eternal relationships with many.

You never need to worry about losing a friend by sharing with them the principles of the gospel. True friends will not be offended. If they are not interested in learning about the Church, they will tell you so.

Over the past twenty-four years, I have been asked by many close friends to invest my time and money into multi-level marketing opportunities. Some friends were more aggressive in their approach than others. With each opportunity, my answer was always the same—not interested. I was content with my current profession and didn't have a desire to branch out to something else, even if it did bring additional income. I didn't fault them for approaching me; I respected them. I never lost a friend by refusing to grasp hold of their ideas or opportunities.

Sharing the gospel with friends and associates will never hinder a relationship. If they are not ready to hear about the gospel, they will tell you so. If they are not ready today, it doesn't mean they won't be ready someday. In other words, don't totally give up if they decline your offer. Continue to be the good friend that you are and follow the Spirit. If they are ready, they will welcome the gospel into their heart and prepare themselves for baptism.

Doing missionary work while on the road is easy, fun and rewarding. During the summer of 2001, my good friend (Ron Johnson) and I took our two sons (Tyson and Shawn) to Alaska for their senior trip. Our itinerary called for fishing, fishing and more fishing. Our thoughts were centered on three bodies of water; Russian River, Kenai River and Cook Inlet. Our only desire was to enjoy some time with our sons and return home with hundreds of pounds of salmon and halibut.

Once we landed in Alaska, we thought it would be fun to share the gospel with all the waiters and waitresses we came in contact with. We made a game of it and kept track of the number of people we approached. We had fun maneuvering our conversations into a gospel topic. At the conclusion of one particular meal, eighteen-year-old Tyson was rehearsing his line in preparation for sharing the gospel with the waitress. After role-playing his approach with the group, he was ready for the challenge. For some unknown reason, the waitress never returned to our table. After waiting for some time, we approached another employee of the restaurant and solicited his help in finding our waitress. After several more minutes and a call on the PA system, our waitress finally emerged. Standing in the middle of the restaurant with a large platter of food balanced in one hand, our little waitress was going to hear a short message about the Book of Mormon and be invited to learn more about the Church.

Tyson began, "You mentioned to us that you were engaged to be married. Well, we're members of the

Church of Jesus Christ of Latter-day Saints, and we would like to be the first to give you a wedding gift. This card explains a little bit about the Book of Mormon and how it can bless your life. If you call this number, two representatives of the Church will personally bring a copy of the Book of Mormon to your home. We know that this book will bring great happiness in your marriage." The young waitress smiled, said thank you, and placed the pass-a-long card in her pocket.

As we left the restaurant, we all acted like a bunch of anglers who just caught a three hundred-pound halibut. High fives and positive words of encouragement flowed between the four of us. We were excited about our little missionary experience and walked away with feelings of satisfaction and accomplishment.

We may never know the effects our testimony had on this young lady. But we do know that we planted some "gospel seeds" that hopefully one day will be harvested.

We began our trip with the intent to catch a ton of fish. We fished hard for three days, and our efforts only rewarded us with one salmon and two halibut. We were a little disappointed in our fishing experience, but we soon realized that our "fishing trip" was just a by-product of the real purpose of our journey.

Wherever you travel, whomever you meet, opportunities to share the gospel will present itself. Your business trip or journey should always have an additional purpose. Perhaps your business travels are just a by-product of the real reason of your journey.

For verily the voice of the Lord is unto all men, and there is none to escape; and there is no eye that shall not see, neither ear that shall not hear, neither heart that shall not be penetrated. (D&C 1:2)

And the voice of warning shall be unto all people, by the mouths of my disciples, whom I have chosen in these last days. And they shall go forth and none shall stay them, for I the Lord have commanded them. (D&C1:4)

As members of the Church, we are the disciples who will take the gospel message to the world. Missionary work should not be left to the full-time missionaries and general authorities. We are all enlisted in this great work, and each of us must do our part in bringing the gospel message to the world.

We must use good judgment and follow the Spirit when sharing the gospel with those we work with, especially if you're in a managerial position. The gospel message is for all people, but we must use good judgment and find the right time and place when inviting our associates to learn more about the Church. The following stories are a few examples of how this can be accomplished.

A few years ago I was in Salt Lake working with a senior manager of my company. We spent some time in Park City, and the balance of our business was conducted close to Temple Square. I had many opportunities to share the gospel with him, but I didn't want to step out of line. I didn't know what was appropriate behavior. Would he think less of me? Would I offend him?

Once our work was accomplished, we ate dinner and caught a cab back to the airport. As we were walking down the concourse, the senior manager said to me, "You know, Matt, every time I come to Utah, I have this overwhelming feeling of peace come over me." I couldn't take it anymore—I had to say something. I informed him that the feeling he was experiencing was due to the influence of the Church. He stared at me and said, "No, that's not it. I was thinking it had something to do with the mountains." We both broke out in a good laugh. This little exchange of words grew into a wonderful discussion about the Church. The Spirit whispered to me that the time was right to introduce him to the gospel. Over the next hour and a half, I shared with him the basic principles of the gospel and answered his many questions.

The time soon arrived to board the plane. I felt good about our discussion, but I knew that my missionary experience was not complete. To finalize our discussion, I had to extend an invitation for him and his family to learn more about the Church. In the sales industry, we call this the close. It does little to no good to share with a prospective buyer all the features and benefits of a product without asking for the order. If you don't ask for the order, you usually don't get it.

Missionary work is not to be confused with sales. As members of the Church, we don't sell anything. However, the same basic principles of conversation apply. I had to complete our conversation by asking if he would be interested in learning more. I briefly shared my testimony and asked if he and his family would like to learn more about the Church.

I didn't shock him or offend him with my question. Though he wasn't interested in having the missionaries teach his family, he did say that he would like to continue our discussion at a later time. Over the years we have discussed the gospel on many occasions. Though he has not yet joined the Church, he continues to ask questions and enjoys discussing gospel topics.

Five years ago, my family moved into a new subdivision in Puyallup, Washington. We were excited when we learned that four other LDS families also bought homes in our cul-de-sac. Shortly after moving in, a nice-looking middle-aged man with a beard knocked on our door. He informed my wife and me that he was the pastor at the local church and just moved in around the corner. After a little small talk, he handed us a flier and invited us to join him at his Sunday worship service. We graciously declined, welcomed him to the neighborhood and thanked him for introducing himself.

Within a few weeks, we learned that five families in our neighborhood accepted the pastor's offer and eventually joined his church. They joined his congregation because he simply invited them. As members of the Church, sometimes we get too caught up in the fellowshipping aspect of missionary work, when just a simple invitation will do.

On another occasion I was asked to attend a corporate meeting in San Francisco. At one point during the meeting, I came in contact with a young mother from California. During each break I noticed that she spent the entire time talking on the phone. After one particular break, she informed me how much she missed her daughter. It didn't take too long before a discussion on families ensued. Our discussion went from the family to temples to Joseph Smith.

Prior to departing the meeting, I extended an offer for her to learn more about the Church. Without hesitation she said yes. A meeting with the missionaries was arranged, and within four weeks she was baptized.

The reason for the meeting in San Francisco was job-related; however, I believe that the real purpose was to help bring another soul unto Christ.

If you want to have a missionary experience, pray for one. Without fail, the Lord will bless you with an opportunity to share the gospel. Throughout the day, be cognizant of the people you encounter. If the time is right, the Spirit will whisper the words you are to say.

> Therefore, verily I say unto you, lift up your voices unto this people; speak the thoughts that I shall put into your hearts, and you shall not be confounded before men. (D&C 100:5)

As I travel from town to town, I try to stay in hotels that keep a copy of the Book of Mormon in the rooms. I have found that all Marriott-owned establishments, along with a few privately owned motels, do store a copy of the Book of Mormon in the desk or nightstand. Before going to bed on the first night, I take the opportunity to write my testimony in the front of the book. Prior to checking out, I leave a note for the maid along with the copy of the Book of Mormon. To encourage the maid to open the book, I place a small tip at the place where I wrote my testimony. I may never know if any good will ever come from my efforts. But I do know that no good will ever come from no effort.

Always travel with a few tracts, pass-a-long cards and an extra copy of the Book of Mormon. If you don't pack them, you'll never use them.

The purpose for your travel is due to your profession. Perhaps the real reason for your travels are for the Lord. You will never shortchange your company by taking a little extra time to share the gospel. By traveling with your testimony, the Lord will bless you in your profession and in your efforts to share the gospel.

> And if it so be that you should labor all your days in crying repentance unto this people, and bring, save it be one soul unto me, how great shall be your joy with him in the kingdom of my Father!
>
> And now, if your joy will be great with one soul that you have brought unto me into the kingdom of my father, how great will be your joy if you should bring many souls unto me! (D&C 18: 15–16)

Chapter Eight
HONEST IN YOUR DEALINGS

"**A**re you honest in your dealings with your fellowman?" Of all the questions asked during a temple recommend interview, this one is the most difficult for me to answer. The question is so large and touches upon all aspects of life. Is it possible to be totally honest? Can a person be totally honest with their dealings without being perfect? This question has often plagued my soul.

As a young man, I gained a testimony of the importance of home teaching. I love to serve the Lord and found great pleasure in visiting my families. The most difficult part of going home teaching for me is setting the appointment. Over the years, I must admit that I have neglected periodically to set appointments with my families. Because I fail to remember to set the appointment, I didn't follow through with my visits. So what does this have to do with honesty?

At the end of each month, each home teacher gives an accounting of his responsibilities. It's certainly more enjoyable to report 100% home teaching than it is to report 0%. I have been tempted in the past to report a home teaching visit when I knew in my heart that it would be dishonest. Sometimes I would catch myself trying to justify my actions.

Falling short of fulfilling your home teaching responsibilities is a sin of omission. Reporting that you did your home teaching and actually didn't, is a sin of commission. Neglecting to do your home teaching but reporting the truth is a sign of a slothful, but honest person.

We have all experienced bouts of slothfulness. Though we are imperfect from time to time with our actions, we can be perfectly honest in our dealings with our fellowmen. You do not need to be perfect to be completely and totally honest. Honesty and humanity can coexist.

As I consider that temple recommend question, I ponder all the peccadilloes in my character and any major acts of dishonesty. I don't consider myself a dishonest person. I don't take advantage of or cheat people for personal gain. I don't consider myself a liar or deceiver. However, I still feel uncomfortable answering that question in a positive way. To answer that question in an honest way, I answer by admitting that I'm not totally honest. I do make mistakes from time to time with my interactions with others. I don't intentionally mean to hurt or let people down, but I know that I have.

I love the words of Alma as he describes the behavior of the people of Ammon:

> "For they were perfectly honest and upright in all things; and they were firm in the faith of Christ, even unto the end" (Alma 27:27).

> President Hinckley said, "We can only hope there are many in number who are impeccably honest, day in and day out. People who do what they say they will do. People whose word is equal to any bond."

Now that I've admitted that I'm not totally honest, I can only guess that some of you might fall short as well. Honesty is a funny thing. You don't need to be in possession of anything to acquire honesty. To be classified as financially wealthy, you must have money. To be classified as a scholar you must have education. To be classified as a scriptorian, you must have a great knowledge of the scriptures. To be classified as an honest person, all you need is integrity. Someone who possesses integrity will say and do the right thing at all times and in all places. That's all there is to it: just saying and doing the right thing.

Frequently, people will be dishonest in order to protect their interest or cover up their intentions. People use dishonest measures to acquire personal gain and satisfy individual needs. Dishonesty in the workplace is at an all-time high. Pilferage at the retail outlets is astounding. Candidates seeking employment are lying their way into interviews, and many are landing respectable jobs. Some people view dishonesty as a form of persuasive communication and interaction to achieve their objectives.

Once, after interviewing several individuals for a sales position, I narrowed my candidates down to three. I was impressed with all of them, however one young man stood head and shoulders above the rest. I was thoroughly impressed with his resume and the manner in which he conducted himself during the interview. He was what I considered a perfect fit for the job.

Prior to offering him the position, I conducted a background check to verify the validity of his resume and application. I was appalled when I learned that his entire resume was falsified. In a follow-up conversation, I questioned him about the truthful nature of his resume. Without hesitating he said, "I'm sorry I wasted your time, but I lied to you because that was the only way I was going to get the job." My follow-up question to him was, "Did your lying and deceiving get you the job?"

Honesty is one of the great virtues that is becoming lost in today's world. Men and women throughout the world fail to realize how important it is to be honest. Honesty must be a constant behavior. Regardless of the consequence, honesty must prevail. Men and women of integrity cannot walk in crooked paths. Alma said to the people of Gideon:

> For I perceive that ye are in the paths of righteous; I perceive that ye are in the path which leads to the kingdom of God; yea, I perceive that ye are making his paths straight.
>
> …that he cannot walk in crooked paths; neither doth he vary from that which he hath said; neither hath he a shadow of turning from the right to the left, or from that which is right to that which is wrong; therefore, his course is one eternal round. (Alma 7:19–20)

Two of most prevalent forms of dishonesty in the workplace among salespeople are falsification of information and cheating on expense reports. Some people will falsify reports or information to compensate for personal inadequacies or cover up for lack of effort. Those who are dishonest with their expense budgets are cheating their company and actually stealing from the same source that pays their salary.

Some people spend a great deal of time figuring out ways to cheat their company. Finding those little holes where they can skim money for personal gain without working for it or honorably earning it. A great leader once said, "The darkest hour in any man's life is when he sits down to plan how to get money without earning it."

Being dishonest will result in a lose-lose situation. Nothing can be gained, and everything can be lost. Like an obnoxious weed in a manicured garden, sooner or later the dishonest will be discovered, plucked out and disposed of.

A few years ago, I hired a very talented and intelligent young lady. She had all the tools necessary to be successful. Because of her productivity, she was gradually gaining the admiration and respect of her managers and peers. She was so dynamic and talented that she earned the prestigious Presidents Club Award after just one year of service.

Three days after receiving this award, I stumbled upon a significant mistake in her expense report. The word dishonesty never crossed my mind. I sent her a deduction slip along with a little note to pay closer attention to details. She apologized for the oversight and paid the money back. A few months passed and once again I saw the same error. I felt uncomfortable about the situation and conducted my own private investigation. I was devastated when I discovered that she had embezzled thousands of dollars over a twelve-month period. Upon releasing her from her assignment, she told me that she didn't feel bad for what she did, she only felt bad for getting caught.

Dishonesty may have given her twelve-months of additional income, but it robbed her of integrity and a promising future with her company. Integrity is classified as doing the right thing even when nobody is watching.

Late one evening, another sales representative was driving through a vacant parking lot toward his hotel. Upon arrival, he noticed a brown satchel sitting in a grocery cart. Out of curiosity he stopped his car to look into the matter. As he opened the satchel, he saw what appeared to be thousands of dollars in cash. Not knowing what to do, he took the money to his hotel room and counted every dollar. Several thoughts crossed his mind as he counted out the money. Why was that satchel in a grocery cart? Where did it come from? Whose money was it? Of all the thoughts that entered his mind, taking the money for his gain was not one of them.

This sales representative may not be a perfect individual, but he is a man of integrity. Even though he was going through personal financial difficulty and could have desperately used the money, he did the right thing by contacting the local authorities. It was discovered that a convenience store close by was robbed just hours before the satchel was discovered.

President Hinckley said, "In our day, those found in dishonesty aren't put to death, but something within them dies. Conscience chokes, character withers, self-respect vanishes, and integrity dies. Without honesty, our lives disintegrate into ugliness, chaos, and a lack of any kind of security and confidence."

We live in a world where dishonesty runs rampant. Personal identities are being stolen along with life savings.

Retail prices continue to rise due to shoplifting. Many students are cheating their way through college. Applications for employment are falsified. Even athletic standards and expectations have increased due to dishonesty.

Over the past several years, a family friend has struggled to secure a full time position on a major league baseball team. Since his mission, he has been traded to four different teams. He has paid his dues and has proven that he is capable of a starting position. His skills are superior to most athletes playing his position. The only weak area in his repertoire is his power at the plate. The interesting fact is that his strength and power is quite adequate. However, compared to others at his same position, he lags a little behind.

Dishonesty in the world of sports comes in the form of unauthorized uses of drugs and performance enhancers. Records are falling at an alarming rate. The honest athlete is finding it difficult to compete with the dishonest. Because of dishonesty and the illegal use of drugs, standards and expectations are raised beyond the ability of the natural athlete.

In the field of sports or business, the dishonest will never prevail. Honesty is indeed the best policy.

"To thine own self be true; and it must follow as the night and the day, thou canst not then be false to any man" (Hamlet).

More people lose their jobs due to dishonesty than inadequacy. Whether a little white lie or a major infraction, corporate America seldom tolerates a dishonest person. Admitting fault and acknowledging mistakes is not a sign of weakness, but rather a symbol of integrity.

> "Honesty is the cornerstone of all success, without which confidence and ability to perform shall cease to exist." —Mary Kay Ash

Recently, I terminated one of my most productive sales representatives because of dishonesty. Her years of experience and success could not compensate for her sporadic spells of dishonesty. She never fell prey to the large infractions; it was the little white lies that eventually caught up with her.

Many people will admit that it is morally wrong to be dishonest in big things yet feel comfortable engaging in little acts of dishonesty. Is there really any difference between dishonesty involving a stolen car or a stolen book? Is there any difference in principle between a little white lie and a major act of perjury? Regardless how big or how small, a lie is just that, a lie. You can never live it down. You can never ignore it because it will be engraved upon your conscience. Lying and deceiving not only affects your relationship with your peers and superiors but will tarnish your relationship with the Lord.

The following guidelines will help you remain honest in your dealings with your fellowmen.

1. Say what you know. Don't say what you think, and don't say what you feel. If you don't know, say so. You will be respected and trusted by your customers, peers and superiors if you are forthright with your interactions and conversations.

2. Don't embellish the truth. It's better to understate the facts than it is to exaggerate the truth. It's never a compliment to be known as an exaggerator. You can be interesting and have a sense of humor without embellishing the truth.

3. Don't grandstand or promenade your accomplishments. Be humble and acknowledge the support of those around you.

4. Never accept undue credit. The person who willingly gives credit to another receives credibility in return.

5. Treat the company's funds as if they were your own. Don't stay in glamorous hotels and eat at expensive restaurants just because you can. Be accurate with company funds and never falsify your expense report. Make sure you can account for every dollar. Be wise and never abuse or misuse your travel budget or other corporate funds.

6. Be loyal in your labors and work an honest day. Never shortchange your company by cutting corners or using company time for personal activities.

7. Never falsify reports or information. The information you provide is a reflection of your standards. Be honest, accurate and complete, as you're only as good as your word.

President Kimball said, "Where there is no integrity, there is no character, and this quality is indispensable."

Abraham Lincoln once said, "I am not bound to win, but I am bound to be true; I am not bound to succeed, but I am bound to live by the light that I have."

The Thirteenth Article of Faith states,

"We believe in being honest, true, chaste, benevolent, virtuous, and in doing good to all men...."

This is our motto, our creed, our standard of excellence and our belief.

The honest will prevail in their pursuit of excellence as the dishonest will fail and suffer the consequences of their actions. Be honest in your dealings with your fellowmen.

"Lying lips are an abomination to the Lord: but they that deal truly are his delight." (Proverbs 12:22)

Chapter Nine
FINAL APPROACH
"RETURN WITH HONOR"

"**H**ouston, we have a problem." On Saturday, April 11, 1970, Apollo 13 was launched into space. Three fine astronauts; James A. Lovell, Jr.; John L. Swigert, Jr.; and Fred W. Haise, Jr., were about to become the third crew to land on the moon. Thousands of hours of preparation and planning were invested to assure the safety of the spacecraft and crew. Their mission had a significant purpose and anything short of accomplishing their goals would result in failure.

On April 13, 1970, just fifty-six hours into the mission, a routine procedure turned into a devastating experience. At 10:06 PM, the power fans were turned on within the tank. The exposed fan wires shorted, and the teflon insulation caught fire. The fire spread along the wires to the electrical conduit in the side of the tank, causing the number-two oxygen tank to explode. The explosion damaged the number-one tank and parts of the interior of the service module. The normal supply of electricity, light and water was lost. The crew was two hundred thousand miles from earth and their Command Module was beginning to fall apart.

The focus of the mission suddenly changed. No one cared any longer about a successful lunar landing and scientific exploration. The massive amount of time and money invested was no longer important. Bringing those three men home safe and alive was the only thing that mattered. Anything short of their safety would be a tragedy.

Men and women back at Mission Control worked around the clock to find a way to circumvent the problem. Millions of prayers were offered from all parts of the world. As Americans, we wanted only one thing—our boys to return safely home.

On April 17, 1970, shortly after 1:00 PM EST, those three astronauts completed their journey and made it safely back to earth. Tears of emotion and prayers of thanksgiving were uttered by millions. Those fine men did not return home as failures. In fact, they returned with honor. They battled through a myriad of problems and obstacles. Through it all, they kept focused and positive. They didn't give up, and their mission was not in vain. Their mission was an example to us all that we, too, can overcome the obstacles, the negatives, the problems and even the Adversary.

As you depart your homes and leave your families, never lose sight of the ultimate goal of returning with honor. Your spouse and children do care about your successes away from home, but not nearly as much as they care about your safe return. Returning with honor means to return clean, virtuous and unscathed from the negative and impure effects of the world.

TRANSITION

Depending on the length of time away from home, your transition back to normal family life will vary. The longer you are away from home, the longer it can take to transition back. It's always interesting to watch as astronauts take their first few steps after a long journey in space. The absence of gravity is evident in the way they walk and utilize their other motor skills. It takes a little time to adjust back to earth life and the natural pull of gravity.

The same holds true for the Road Warrior. Like the astronaut, you too experienced your own lack of gravity. Throughout the duration of your travels, you are not tied down to family, church or civic responsibilities. You are not pulled in different directions. You have become somewhat self-absorbed as you focus all your energies on yourself and the things you need to accomplish. In a way, your journey enabled you to enjoy mental, physical and emotional weightlessness. Though you missed your loved ones, you still enjoyed the tranquility during those peaceful evening and morning hours.

Being a father of six, I yearned for the moment when I would walk into my home after a long business trip and hear those precious words, "Daddy's home." The little pitter-patter of feet coming from all corners of the home was music to my ears. I would throw my little children high in the air and hug them tightly. I would embrace my teenagers and then give my wife a long passionate kiss. Life was great, and I was happy to be home. Unfortunately, my welcome-home party didn't always turn out the way I planned.

After one extremely stressful business trip, I was eager to get home to the people who loved me most. The week was difficult, and my patience and tolerance for trials and tribulations was shot. I was exhausted and I needed my home and family to reassure me that life was still worth living. It was dinnertime, and I could almost smell the aroma of fresh-baked bread and homemade chicken and dumpling soup. It was finally my time to receive a little tender loving care.

As I pulled into the driveway, I saw a clutter of bikes near the front porch, eight in all. This was not a good sign of things to come. Children that I didn't even know were running in and out the front door. One of our finest quilts was lying in the mud. I noticed a significant scratch on the passenger side door of our new car. As I entered my home, I was greeted by the shrills of children screaming at the top of their lungs and running like a bunch of wild animals throughout the house. My little sanctuary was unkempt and disorderly. I thought to myself, "this is matter unorganized." Or at least it appeared that way.

My wife sat me down and reassure me that our home wasn't out of control. The only thing that had changed was me. She would calmly ask me to take some time and relax as I transitioned back to family life. My home wasn't really as bad as it appeared; it just seemed that way to me.

I learned early on in our marriage that my responsibilities don't end once I enter the walls of my home. My responsibilities only change. I learned to quickly transition from the traveling businessman to husband and father. Knowing full well that my most important responsibilities were that of husband and father to my most precious possessions, my family.

The best part of the week is returning home. Everybody is happy to see you and wants your attention. You are a celebrity in your own environment. You must learn to adjust quickly from hotel life to home life. The adjustment must start and finish before you return home.

Prior to walking through your front door, make sure you give thanks to Heavenly Father for your safe travels and the safety of your family. Pray for patience and understanding. Condition yourself to be tolerant through the transition period. I often conduct a little interview with my mind; I call it a check-up from the neck up. I remind myself that I'm entering the best place on earth. The most important people in my life reside within the walls of my home. Be grateful to be home and bask in the outpouring of love that your family will bestow upon you.

EPILOGUE

Prior to my son leaving the Mission Training Center and reporting to the Chile Santiago West Mission, he wrote me a letter that changed my outlook on obedience. He shared with me the following experience:

" . . . I was having a difficult time learning the language and memorizing my discussions. One of my instructors came to me and asked if I was obeying all the mission rules. I thought for a second and responded, 'Yes, I believe I am.'

She then said, 'Are you sure you are obeying all the mission rules?'

I thought a little harder and said, 'Yes, I'm pretty sure I'm obeying all the mission rules.'

She concluded by saying, 'Well then, you have no need to worry.'

"That night it dawned on me that I wasn't obeying all the rules. There is this rule in the Mission Training Center that you must have a part in your hair. Yeah right, me have a part? No way! After I thought about it for a while, I realized that I wasn't obeying all the rules. Regardless how big or small a rule might seem, I knew I had to obey all of them. After taking my shower the following morning, I put a part in my hair.

"Later that morning I experienced something that I never experienced before in my life. I saw an immediate blessing as a result of obedience. I was speaking with a native Chilean and could actually communicate with him. It was a miracle! I understood him, and he understood me. The key to success and happiness in life is obedience." —Elder Shawn McNaughton

President Hinckley said, "Be true to your convictions. You know what is right, and you know what is wrong. You know when you are doing the proper thing. You know when you are giving strength to the right cause. Be loyal. Be faithful. Be true."

By following the principles and guidelines shared in this book, you can avoid the turbulence of the Adversary while traveling away from home and family.

You do have the ability to hear the voice of the Lord. You can safeguard your soul by putting on the armor of God. You can keep yourself unspotted from the world. You can avoid the pitfalls and temptations of the hotel. You can remain morally clean while working with the opposite sex. You can obey the Word of Wisdom and keep your body physically fit. You can honor and fulfill your church and family commitments. You can be a missionary by traveling with your testimony. You can be honest with your dealings and loyal in your labors.

For verily I say unto you, blessed is he that keepeth my commandment, whether in life or in death; and he that is faithful in tribulation, the reward of the same is greater in the kingdom of heaven. (D&C 58:2)

Welcome home thou good and faithful servant!

Matthew McNaughton is an accomplished motivational speaker. He has addressed both LDS and non-LDS audiences around the country. His message on "Avoiding the turbulence of the Adversary while traveling away from home and family" is a critical and timely message in today's troubled world. For more information about McNaughton's publications and services, including information regarding seminars, firesides and courses for the general public, please send email to: roadwarriorinfo@hotmail.com